THE
DIVINE
GOVERNMENT

ALSO BY HELENA ROERICH

Agni Yoga Series

Leaves of Morya's Garden I
Leaves of Morya's Garden II
New Era Community
Agni Yoga
Infinity I
Infinity II
Hierarchy
Heart
Fiery World I
Fiery World II
Fiery World III
Aum
Brotherhood
Supermundane I
Supermundane II
Supermundane III

Agni Yoga: The High Path
On Eastern Crossroads
Foundations of Buddhism
Letters of Helena Roerich
At the Threshold of the New World

THE
DIVINE GOVERNMENT
GUIDANCE FOR THE LEADER

HELENA ROERICH

Radiant Books
New York

Translation, Introduction, Glossary
© 2023, 2025 by Alexander Gerasymchuk

Guidance for the Leader was originally compiled by Helena Roerich in 1933 as *Naputstviye Vozhdyu*. Translated from the Russian by Alexander Gerasymchuk, Joanna Dobson, and John Woodsworth.

Helena Roerich's original letters to Franklin D. Roosevelt are housed in the Franklin D. Roosevelt Presidential Library and Museum in Hyde Park, New York.

This book was previously published in 2023 as *The Secret World Government: Cosmic Guidance for the Leader*.

All rights reserved. No part of this book may be used or reproduced in any manner whatsoever without written permission from the publisher except in the case of brief quotations embodied in critical articles and reviews. For additional information, please contact *info@radiantbooks.co*.

Library of Congress Control Number: 2025939507

Published in 2025 by Radiant Books
radiantbooks.co

ISBN 978-1-63994-058-5 (hardback)
ISBN 978-1-63994-057-8 (paperback)
ISBN 978-1-63994-032-5 (e-book)

CONTENTS

Introduction: The Divine Government . . . . . . *vii*

Letters to Franklin D. Roosevelt 1
Guidance for the Leader 21

Glossary. *105*
About the Author *151*

∽

Introduction

THE DIVINE GOVERNMENT

AMIDST THE VAST ARRAY of myths and legends passed down through the ages, there is one that has fascinated all the peoples of the world from ancient times to the present day. It tells of a mysterious kingdom, a true paradise, surrounded by the snow-capped peaks of majestic and inaccessible mountains, home only to immortal Sages, pure in heart and enlightened in spirit. Having supernatural powers, these Beings rule everything invisibly, making crucial decisions concerning the destiny of humanity, directing its evolution in accordance with the just Laws of the Cosmos and saving humankind when, like a small unthinking child, it walks up to the edge of an abyss.

This most secret of places on Earth is guarded by mysterious powers that prevent unbidden guests from discovering it, even with the help of the most advanced technology. Indeed, the inhabitants of this Sacred Land of the Gods have spiritual powers in comparison with which all the advances of humanity appear as children's toys.

Shambhala, Agartha, the Garden of Eden, the Pure Land, Shangri-La — endless are the names given to this Stronghold of Light, located in the heart of the Himalayas. It has stood indestructible since the dawn of time, rising like a White Island above the raging waves of earthly life. Indeed, bottomless seas and oceans separate the Realm of Radiant Spirits from the lands of ignorant children. And this special Island will remain undiscovered until human eyes are able to withstand, unblinded, the Light of Divine Truth.

Ancient knowledge of the existence of the Spiritual Brotherhood is reflected in all world religions: Angelic Orders in Christianity, Judaism, and Islam, Bodhisattvas in Buddhism, and the pantheon of Gods in Hinduism. In the Bible, this Hierarchy of Light is also represented as Jacob's Ladder that connects the Earth to the Heavens, along which Angels ascend and descend.

It is in this realm that the true World Government assembles, serving the ideals of the Common Good alone. Its decisions and activities are always aimed at helping, uniting, and saving peoples as well as the entire planet Earth. And although this Government is otherworldly in nature, it has often offered its help to various national leaders, the acceptance of which has led to unprecedented prosperity, its rejection, to decline or oblivion.

On this subject, Helena Roerich explained: "Perhaps, some are confused by the definition of the Hierarchy as the World Government, and a Secret one to boot? But what else is one to call the great invisible Care, Guidance, and Help received, without falling into ecclesiastical terminology?

"How would you name and explain the repeated and attested appearances of Saints to their followers, after they have relinquished their earthly form, in order to warn them of danger or to give useful advice? ... One may cite innumerable manifestations of the Great Guidance of this light-bearing Host of the Hierarchy throughout all ages and all peoples. Therefore, rejoice in your heart, for, truly, the Hierarchy of Light represents the Fathers and Brothers of all humanity. Let your heart not be troubled by new names of the most ancient concepts. New definitions are more accessible to the younger generations."[1]

And further in the words of the Great Lord of Shambhala:

"Urusvati[2] explained to many why We are called the World Government. Indeed, each person, to varying degrees, senses

---

[1] Helena Roerich, *Pis'ma* [Letters], vol. 6 (Moscow: Mezhdunarodnyy tsentr Rerikhov, 2006), p. 387.

[2] Helena Roerich's spiritual name.

that the focus of Knowledge is located somewhere. Where there is Knowledge, there is Power. It is not without reason that some people dream of Us, but others hate Us and would seek to destroy Our Abode.

"In world events, observers may notice something beyond human logic. Even Our own devotees many times have accused Us of procrastination and indifference, but such hasty accusers saw only one aspect of events. They could not know the causes and effects. They could not compare the incoming circumstances. They could not foresee when precisely the decisive blow must manifest. Who can know the Plan and the steps that lead to it?

"According to their partial understanding, people insist on their own measures, but Our disciples never forcibly suppress the decision of the Teacher. They understand how to harmonize their free will with Our decision. One must have great balance in order to recognize the reasonableness of Our Guidance without crippling one's own free will. We care hugely about this decision. The best leaders of nations had this balance which made it easier for Us to impart Our decisions to them. …

"Marks of Our Guidance can be found all over the world. Some exalted persons accepted it, but pitiful parodies of monarchs rejected Our Counsels and thereby plunged their countries into misery. However, even these situations We turn to the good. You are already familiar with thoughts on *Tactica Adversa*.

"We may recall how, before the great war, a certain arrogant monarch received Our warning, but preferred to lose his throne and disregarded Our Command. Likewise, another head of state would not hear out Our Ambassador preferring to plunge his country into turmoil.

"We cannot say that in ancient times We gave Commands more often or that there are many of them now, but the human ear is as deaf as it ever was.

"We stand guard to protect the World."[1]

"People generally do not like to have something special around them. Thus, much that could be useful in Our work is rejected.

"And We had to act under the most ordinary appearances. We even had to bear conventional titles, so that it would be easier to penetrate environments that were the most closed and lost.

"We constantly take care that each impact occurs at the right time. If Our adversaries involve the world in turmoil and even war, We must foresee that the consequences of events will be beneficial to peoples and their prosperity. This is why We are called the World Government. People are afraid of such names, yet they themselves willingly pray to the Highest Concept and are ready to accept its Hand. If you imagine the Highest Concept and have living faith in it, then why can you not also imagine the World Government? Thus you can manifest reverence for the Highest Concept of the Hierarchy."[2]

Without delving too deep into times past, let us embark on a journey through the pages of unknown history that mark the Guidance of Shambhala.

In the 10th century, before accepting Christianity, the Grand Prince of Kyiv, Volodymyr, studied long and hard the question of which religion to choose for his people, negotiating with representatives of various faiths. A monk named Sergius recounted to Prince Volodymyr an ancient legend about Shambhala, known among the Slavic peoples as *Belovodye*, the Land of White Waters. Inspired by the story, the prince entrusted Sergius to go to the East in search of the Kingdom of which he spoke.

---

[1] Helena Roerich, *Agni Yoga s kommentariyami* [Agni Yoga with comments], vol. 2 (Moscow: Eksmo, 2010), pp. 750–751.

[2] Roerich, *Agni Yoga s kommentariyami*, p. 782.

After several years of seeking, the monk ended up alone. Completely exhausted, still he continued on his way until the people guarding the borders of Shambhala found him and led him there. After his return, Father Sergius, like everyone who visited the Land of the Gods, took a vow of silence, which could be broken only before death in order to entrust the secret legend to the next carrier of the mystery. Twenty-seven times the secret was transmitted by word of mouth, before it was finally written down in 1893. And only 950 years later, in 1943, was the vow of silence finally removed and the story published in a Russian-language newspaper in the United States, revealing what Father Sergius had seen in the Kingdom of White Waters. He also received a prophecy for the long-suffering people of Kyivan Rus' — modern Ukraine.[1]

In the Middle Ages, the peoples of Europe believed that somewhere far away in the East reigned a mysterious Christian ruler, Prester John, whose lineage went back to the ancient Magi who brought gifts to the newborn Christ. This belief was also strengthened because in the 12th century the head of an unknown state in Asia began sending letters to a number of Christian monarchs: Manuel I Komnenos, Frederick I Barbarossa, Louis VII, and others.

But one of the most guarded pages of history associated with the name of Prester John is his arrival in Rome in 1122 for a personal meeting with Pope Callixtus II, which was a significant event not only for the Roman Curia, but also for all of Italy.[2] Perhaps somewhere in the secret library of the Vatican there is a more detailed description of this meeting than the one we know of today.

Subsequently, the Popes made a number of attempts to establish contact with Prester John. In 1177, Pope Alexander III

---

[1] See *The Kingdom of White Waters* (New York: Radiant Books, 2022).

[2] See Keagan Brewer, *Prester John: The Legend and its Sources* (Farnham: Ashgate, 2015), pp. 34–38.

sent his doctor Philip from Venice as an ambassador with a letter to John, "beloved in Christ the son, illustrious and magnificent king of the Indians," in which he urged the Prester to join Catholicism and asked him to send a letter of reply with the ambassadors.[1] In the 13th century, Pope Innocent IV sent three missions to Asia, whose task aside from converting the Mongols to the Christian faith was the secret assignment to find the mysterious kingdom of Prester John. Of course, they did not find it, because only one who is invited or who truly needs help and advice can enter the Kingdom, and not one who comes for the sake of curiosity or who would attempt to convert its inhabitants to some other faith.

Nevertheless, as everything in our dual world has its polar opposite, so the spiritual Hierarchy of Light is confronted by the shadow government of evil forces, about which there are many conspiracy theories. The shadow government strives for world domination, often following only one principle: "divide and conquer." From centuries past, their servants have penetrated the environment of religious ministers in order to distort beyond recognition the simple and pure commandments of the spiritual teachings of all peoples and ages. This accounts for the emergence of the dogmas and terrible fanaticism, which resulted in cruel intolerance and the persecution of all dissidents and infidels, contrary to the instructions of Christ, Muhammad, Buddha, and other Teachers of love and mercy for all. But, of course, one of the main tasks of the forces of evil is to convince people that such forces do not really exist, because once people deny something, they stop being wary of it and fall more easily into the traps cleverly prepared for their minds.

At the present time, equipped with huge financial resources, the dark government is attempting to destructively

---

[1] Brewer, *Prester John*, p. 94.

influence the policy of earthly leaders, instigating conflicts and bloody wars on religious, political, or any other grounds, hiding behind "good intentions." After all, they know the sacred power of blood, which can be turned into evil. Their networks unite the most diverse categories of people. In order to undermine everything from within, their representatives are disguised not only behind the mask of politicians and financiers, but also behind the cassocks of priests, behind the costumes of philanthropists, and in leadership positions of organizations designed to serve the ideals of the Light. They know neither national borders nor laws, and their minions may be implacable enemies in public, but will shake hands with each other behind the scenes. They have reached perfection in the development of technologies for manipulating human psychology in order to pass off black for white, and they skilfully use this to achieve their destructive goals in different countries.

They did everything possible to ridicule and slander those who brought the Message from Shambhala into the world, such as Helena Blavatsky. These messengers implemented the Great Plan to unite the peoples of the Earth into one single family of humanity by spreading the Light of Divine Knowledge and Wisdom.

The Invisible Government of the Forces of Light chooses the most worthy individuals for its mission of helping humanity, since the dwellers of this Hidden Mountainous Country very rarely go beyond its borders due to the suffocating and poisoned atmosphere of the lowlands. Many of these chosen individuals have remained unknown to the world, but some names have been written into the pages of history books nevertheless, albeit shrouded in a variety of secrets, legends, and myths.

Of course, the most famous of these is the mysterious Count of Saint-Germain, or Mahatma Rakoczy, who appeared in different centuries, during the reign of different kings, remaining forever young. The Count represents the Protector of America and Europe, and is now working to save our planet from destruction.

His advice was heeded by the founding fathers of the United States, George Washington and Benjamin Franklin, and he played a decisive role in the adoption of the Declaration of Independence of the United States in 1776.[1]

He also attempted to implement the idea of the United States of Europe. It is well known that Saint-Germain met with Louis XVI and Marie Antoinette, whom he advised to initiate just reforms in France in order to prevent a future revolutionary explosion. They did not heed his warnings, and the revolution resulted in a period of mass terror. To put an end to terror in France and to all bloody wars between European countries, Saint-Germain proposed a plan to unite Europe. His plan failed at this time, but his idea and dream of a united Europe nevertheless found its reflection 200 years later in the form of the European Union.

On behalf of Shambhala, the Count of Saint-Germain also visited Russia on more than one occasion to carry out a historical mission. He met with the young Mikhail Kutuzov, the future commander-in-chief who defeated Napoleon. Kutuzov accepted the instructions of Saint-Germain, thereby ensuring unprecedented success that accompanied him in spite of many difficulties. Saint-Germain also met with Count Vorontsov, through whom he passed a warning to the Decembrists.

In her letters, Helena Roerich writes: "Saint-Germain played a role in Russian history, too. It was with his help that Catherine the Great ascended the Russian throne. I am aware of the conclusions and prophecies that Saint-Germain made

---

[1] The speech delivered by the Count of Saint-Germain immediately before the signing of the Declaration of Independence decided America's destiny. To read this electrifying speech, visit radiantbooks.co/bonus.

during his stay in the Russian capital. They are far from flattering, and, therefore, this is not the time to publish them. ...

"Vorontsov was one of a group of Russians at Catherine's court who, after meeting with the Count of Saint-Germain, turned to the Teaching of Life. Alien to military affairs, Vorontsov left the service and followed Saint-Germain. As a foreigner, he helped Saint-Germain depart France. Truly, Vorontsov was in great danger when, taking advantage of his resemblance to Saint-Germain, he took on his appearance and thereby incurred the persecution that was intended for Saint-Germain. Of course, the Great Brothers remember those who helped Them and were exposed to danger for Their sake. Therefore, Vorontsov arrived with Saint-Germain in India. One can only imagine how close he was able to get to the Stronghold of Light! However, three circumstances brought him back to his homeland. Firstly, his excessive passion for the rites of magic; secondly, his attachment to his relatives; and thirdly, when it became clear that he could not stay in India without harm to his spiritual development, he was entrusted to warn the Decembrists of their wrongful mission.

"The Vorontsov family preserved the memory of the strange ancestor who disappeared, but since everything surrounding the Great Brotherhood is associated with the label of charlatanism, Vorontsov's name was placed somewhere between the mystics and the quacks. Some of his letters remained held at the Public Library in Saint Petersburg, but others were subsequently retrieved. In any case, Vorontsov was one of the few who knew about the Himalayan Brotherhood and who disseminated information about the Mahatmas. In the private archive of the Viceroy to the Caucasus, Vorontsov-Dashkov, letters were found that made mention of the Teachers of India. And the family archives of the Fadeyevs, relatives of H. P. Blavatsky, stored curious documents concerning Vorontsov. I also had a ritual dagger that belonged to

Vorontsov, and, in my childhood, I loved to repeat excerpts from the ritual chants that he brought back from India, and which somehow reached my family. Of course, there was no one left who could remember their origin or meaning."[1]

There is also evidence that Abraham Lincoln announced the Emancipation Proclamation on 1 January 1863, because he received a message from the Secret Government of Shambhala in the most unusual and startling way. That message goes as follows:

"There is in the spirit world a congress of wise spirits who hold the welfare of this nation in their keeping. You, sir, have been called to your present position to serve a great and mighty purpose. There are today thousands who are in physical bondage, from whose neck the yoke of oppression must be lifted, that this republic may lead the world. Thou art the man!

"Issue, we implore you, a proclamation of emancipation giving freedom to the slave and from that hour victory will crown the Union Army and heaven and humanity will be served."[2]

This prediction came true, and after the Proclamation was issued, all battles were successful on the Union side.

Unfortunately, national rulers more often than not lacked the wisdom to heed the advice transmitted to them from the Abode of the Mahatmas — the Great Souls.

So, in 1851, Mahatma Morya, who in 1924 became the new head of the Government of Shambhala, personally arrived in London as a member of a delegation from India to meet with Queen Victoria. At that time, he also had his very first meeting with Helena Blavatsky in Hyde Park, at which he outlined her future mission. The purpose of his visit to the Queen

---

[1] Roerich, *Pis'ma*, vol. 4 (Moscow: Mezhdunarodnyy tsentr Rerikhov, 2002), pp. 433–434.

[2] "Was Lincoln Guided by the Higher Masters?" *Liberation*, vol. 2 (February 1932), p. 379. To read this article, visit radiantbooks.co/bonus.

was to warn the monarch that if Great Britain did not change its policy towards its vast colonies, in particular India, nothing would remain of it but an island. The thing is, a mystical union exists between Great Britain and India, as that between a man and a woman, where India was in the role of the oppressed wife, deprived of her rights. However, only equality between these two countries could qualitatively transform the British Empire, which occupied one quarter of Earth's land surface, and preserve it to this day. Nevertheless, a different choice was made — hence the cause of the collapse of the Empire in the mid-20th century was sown almost 100 years earlier, when the Higher Assistance was rejected by the Queen.

Sorry examples can be cited from the very recent past, in the 20th century. In 1926, the Ambassadors of Shambhala, Helena and Nicholas Roerich, arrived in Moscow, "the nest of madness,"[1] to pass the warning and advice of the Mahatmas to Joseph Stalin. But instead of receiving them, the authorities ordered them to be arrested, and only a miracle prevented them from being imprisoned. The best opportunities for building a just state on the territory of the USSR were missed, and instead there followed mass murder, repressions, torture of the people, and the suppression of any manifestation of free will.

In the same way, in 1927, the Roerichs delivered a message to Tibet to help it avoid the land's impending difficult fate. But again, the Roerichs were not even permitted as far as the doorstep, having been detained in conditions of hunger and cold for half a year among the snowbound mountains — circumstances that undermined the health of many of the exhibition's members. At that time the Lord of Shambhala suggested to the Roerichs that they write the following to the government of Tibet:

---

[1] Helena Roerich, *Zapisi Ucheniya Zhivoy Etiki* [Records of the Teaching of Living Ethics], vol. 8 (Moscow, 2010), p. 8.

"While crossing the border of Tibet, let us write approximately as follows:

"The Great Lama, who came from the mountains, told us:

"'Before the great time of Maitreya, let Tibet be given the opportunity to strengthen and purify the great Teaching of the Blessed Buddha. As indicated in the prophecies, you will come from the West and bring the sign of dignity, offerings, and a new unity of the Teaching. If Lhasa accepts this sign of testing, the time of Maitreya will not bypass Tibet. But if unification with the believers of the West is rejected, then your every burden will fall on the head of Tibet, and Tibet will lose its freedom and the purity of the Teaching. May the prophecies be fulfilled!

"'What has been said is as true as it is that the prophecy of Great Shambhala lies under the cornerstone of Ghoom!'

"In fulfilling the instructions of the Great Lama, we brought friendship and wealth to Tibet, but were received as bandits. We passed through twenty-four countries and brought the Light of the Teaching through many dangers. May the prophecy be fulfilled! May a new stream of the Teaching shine!

"What has been said is as true as it is that the prophecy of Great Shambhala lies under the cornerstone of Ghoom!"[1]

Yet the officials of Tibet remained deaf to the message from Shambhala and a quarter of a century later, as a result of this refusal, a grievous fate befell the people of Tibet.

In 1928, the Lord of Shambhala said: "Now the lamas have not realized Our message"; "Tibet must live out its fate."[2] And then later, in 1932, He added: "Russia, of course, is rolling in the direction We have indicated. This is her own fault, as is the case with Tibet. We are obliged to give warning, but disobedience brings consequences."[3]

---

[1] Roerich, *Zapisi Ucheniya Zhivoy Etiki*, vol. 8, pp. 170–171.

[2] Roerich, *Zapisi Ucheniya Zhivoy Etiki*, vol. 8, pp. 303, 450.

[3] Roerich, *Zapisi Ucheniya Zhivoy Etiki*, vol. 12 (Wismar, 2011), p. 217.

Likewise, President Herbert Hoover rejected the advice of the Lord of Shambhala, although it could have helped him prevent the stock market crash of 1929, which resulted in grave economic crisis — the Great Depression. After all, the Roerichs' colleagues learned from the Teacher in 1928 of the forthcoming difficulties in the country.[1]

However, one should note a positive example that took place in the 20th century. In 1934 the help of Shambhala was again offered to America through Helena Roerich, who entered into correspondence with President Franklin D. Roosevelt.

In her letters, Roerich warned Roosevelt of the danger of Germany so that the United States could prepare for the coming world war. The President would ask Roerich questions that troubled him and receive answers to them. Thanks to the fact that Roosevelt partially accepted the advice given through her, he was able to solve a number of problems in his country. This enabled him to become one of America's greatest presidents, along with George Washington and Abraham Lincoln, who in their own time, also accepted guidance from the Secret Government of Shambhala. However, had Roosevelt fully heeded the advice offered to him, there would now be a United States of North and South America.

It is widely known that Adolf Hitler sent at least four expeditions to Tibet under the leadership of Dr. Ernst Schäfer. Along with carrying out traditional scientific research, the expeditions also collected information about various mystical phenomena and objects with mysterious powers, such as the legendary Holy Grail, wanting to strengthen the German army with their help and thereby gain omnipotence. One of the secret tasks entrusted to these expeditions was to find and penetrate Shambhala, to steal the World Treasure guarded there — the Chintamani Stone.

---

[1] See Zinaida Fosdik, *Vospominaniya o Rerikhakh* [Memories of the Roerichs] (Moscow: Eksmo, 2014), pp. 376, 470.

This sacred Stone, which "is also called the Grail,"[1] fell to Earth millions of years ago, as a priceless gift from the constellation of Orion. At the place where the stone hit the surface, Shambhala was founded. The Chintamani carries with it a most powerful cosmic force capable of influencing the entire world. Representatives of the dark forces attempted to take possession of it so as to establish their authority over the planet. By decision of the Council of Shambhala, a fragment, separated from the main body of the Chintamani, which is kept in the Abode of Light, is sent at certain periods to individuals who are to accomplish a special historical mission. It is usually brought by completely unexpected people and methods, but it also disappears in due time in the same unusual manner. The stone has been in the possession of King Solomon, Tamerlane, and Akbar the Great. At the same time, Alexander the Great and Napoleon Bonaparte, to whom the fragment was given, neglected the conditions imposed, and the stone abandoned them, as did their unprecedented luck and success.

In the 20th century, the Chintamani fragment came into the possession of the Roerich family. They received it at Hotel Lord Byron in Paris, France, on 6 October 1923, in a simple mailbox from a Bankers Trust courier. In place of the sender's address read the words: "At the request of M.M." The stone was placed in a casket covered with a piece of leather bearing magical symbols, once owned by King Solomon. The casket was made in Rothenburg in the 13th century, and since then had travelled the world along with a fragment of Orion's gift. The Master explained to the Roerichs that the stone could indeed be used as a weapon capable of sweeping away any enemy, and "neither oceans, nor mountains, nor deserts will be obstacles."[2] But, of course, the Roerichs never used it for such purposes.

---

[1] Wolfram von Eschenbach, *Parzival* (New York: Vintage Books, 1961), p. 252.

[2] Roerich, *Zapisi Ucheniya Zhivoy Etiki*, vol. 4 (Moscow, 2009), p. 100.

Hence Hitler's strong interest in the Chintamani is hardly surprising. So, while travelling across Tibet, Dr. Schäfer and his companions visited ancient monasteries and inquired of the learned lamas about a mysterious country whose inhabitants had exceptional abilities. In one of the monasteries, during a reception held to honour the arrival of the guests from Germany, a monk approached Schäfer and, with the help of an interpreter, told him that they were trying in vain to locate Shambhala, because only those who were invited could find it. He also conveyed a warning to Hitler that he should not start a "great war," since the consequences would be devastating, both for the government and for the entire German people. Interestingly, the members of Schäfer's expedition filmed all the lamas present at the reception, both with film and still cameras. However, in none of the photographs or films was the face of that unusual lama discernible; it appeared always as if shrouded in fog, despite the fact that the faces of the other individuals standing nearby were sharp and clear.

This phenomenon was explained by Mahatma Morya as follows: "So much has been said about the rays that make a person invisible. The next step will be to invent a small device that can always be with you, that makes its carrier invisible. But then Our degree of invisibility remains, when We attract from space certain rays necessary to achieve invisibility; the phenomenon is similar to when certain parts of the body dematerialize."[1]

Where there is the greatest Light, there will be the greatest concentration of the forces of darkness. Thus, the approaches to Shambhala are surrounded by monasteries where dark magic is practised. Many people, inspired by legends to search for this Secret Land, fall into the nets of evil forces offering them an easy way to acquire superhuman abilities, such as clairvoyance and clairaudience, by awakening certain energy centres of the

---

[1] Roerich, *Agni Yoga s kommentariyami*, vol. 2, p. 741.

human body with the help of mechanical techniques, as well as narcotic substances. This is all a destructive road that leads to nowhere, because such abilities must be awakened solely in a natural way, and not artificially.

It is also typical for the dark forces to employ the signs and symbols of Shambhala, acting under the "guise of light," going as far as to use very name *Shambhala*, in order to desecrate them in some way in the eyes of the masses, who will not delve into the details. Hitler appropriated the oldest symbol of Life, the swastika, for use in Nazi emblems. Since then, for many people, this solar symbol has been associated solely with Nazi atrocities, and not with well-being. Incidentally, the earliest known image of the swastika was found in Ukraine.[1] However, anyone who uses something so sacred to cover their dark deeds always fails, because sooner or later it will turn against them.

One more example is the number 24, which is sacred to Shambhala and the Masters. They especially celebrate the 24th day of every month, and in the 24th year of each century the Great Council of Shambhala assembles. So why should not the dark forces instil in someone the need for "special military operations" to be started precisely on 24 March 1999 or 24 February 2022, so that the millions of those affected would never again associate "twice the sacred macrocosmic number"[2] 24 with something good and positive, as was the case with the swastika?

Thus, Hitler's expedition managed to find the remnants of a sect of dark sorcerers. They possessed the secrets of hypnosis and could kill with a single glance. But eventually they were defeated after special dogs were trained that were impervious

---

[1] Joseph Campbell, *The Flight of the Wild Gander* (Novato, CA: New World Library, 2002), p. 117.

[2] H. P. Blavatsky, "The Six-pointed and Five-pointed Stars," *Collected Writings*, vol. 3 (Wheaton, IL: Theosophical Publishing House, 1966), p. 320.

to hypnosis. These few sorcerers were taken to Germany in order to employ their powers towards influencing the rulers of countries against which the attack was planned. The sorcerers' influence caused the rulers' consciousness to become confused, which resulted in their taking inadequate decisions. For example, not to react in any way to intelligence data warning them that an invasion was being prepared, as was the case with the leaders of the USSR.

Another mystery associated with the Second World War surrounds the defeat of the Germans near Moscow at the end of 1941. The circumstances were so miraculous that this became one of the great mysteries of history and the stuff of legend. After all, the Germans had all the advantage. There was nothing to prevent them from entering Moscow, whereas the Soviet army and people were drained by Stalin's mass repressions and assassinations; the command of the army was frankly mediocre, as evidenced by the disproportionate losses of the USSR towards the end of the war: approximately 27 million people died, in contrast to approximately 8 million people on the German side.

However, in October 1941, when the Soviet army found itself surrounded near Moscow unable even to delay the lightning-speed offensive of the German troops on the capital, the forces of Nature suddenly entered the battle. It poured with rain and snow. This snatched victory from the hands of the Germans, delaying their movements. The Germans were not prepared for winter conditions, and the operation had to be completed before the first frosts, which began earlier than expected that year. According to the memoirs of the German general, Heinz Guderian,[1] none of the Germans' equipment or weapons were adapted to the terrible cold, and therefore regularly broke down or did not work at all.

---

[1] See Heinz Guderian, *Panzer Leader* (New York: Da Capo Press, 2002), pp. 242–263.

Later, to explain this wonderful natural phenomenon, a legend emerged about Stalin's secret mission according to which, after visiting Saint Matrona of Moscow, he ordered for the plane to circle Moscow with the Icon of the Mother of God, which saved the city.

But prior to this in 1932, the prominent artist Nicholas Roerich painted a prophetic picture dedicated to the Protector of Russia, Saint Sergius of Radonezh, making an inscription at the bottom which ended in three large dots: "St. Reverend Sergius is destined to save the Russian Land three times. The first time was under Prince Dmitry, the second under Minin. The third…"

The notebooks of Helena Roerich, which were kept secret from the public for more than 60 years and revealed only in 2018, contain an explanation of what happened near Moscow. The conversation with Mahatma Morya from the year 1948 indicated that the Great Lord of Shambhala personally intervened in the battle: "Tanks, airplanes, vehicles are stopped by My Ray. They stopped before a new boundary set by My Ray. The new border was needed to affirm the legend of the country's third-time salvation by Sergius of Radonezh. The legend spread all over the country and lent wings to the people. This Ray was the Magnetic Ray of Our Apparatus in the Abode. This Ray is capable of stopping an entire army by paralysing all vehicles and engines."[1]

The natural factor, which is jokingly referred to as "General Frost," is the main reason for the defeat of the Germans near Moscow in 1941. But previously this same "General" decided the outcome of the battles of Charles XII and Napoleon, who launched attacks on Russia in 1708–1709 and 1812, respectively, despite warnings from the Secret Government that they

---

[1] Helena Roerich, "Zapisi besed s Uchitelem (nauchnyye zametki)" [Records of conversations with the Master (scientific notes)], 1948–1950, fol. 25, Roerich Museum, Moscow.

should not take such action. This is how Shambhala guards the chosen lands and peoples who are destined to fulfil a special spiritual mission in the future, despite the fact that these peoples have not yet awakened sufficiently to accomplish it.

When trouble overtakes people, they often complain: if the Higher Powers really exist, then why do they not help? However, the same people again and again push away the outstretched Hand. And after the Higher Assistance is rejected, the Mahatmas no longer have the Cosmic Right to impose themselves, and humanity itself must take steps towards Them for the sake of its own salvation. And no matter how painful it might be for the Masters of Wisdom to watch the consequences unfold, they still cannot violate the free will of humankind by imposing their own will upon them. The only way out is to wait until the existing Karma, which resulted in certain negative consequences, is exhausted although this may take many years, decades, or even centuries.

The question of Karma, or the Law of Cause and Effect, expressed in the formula "as you sow, so shall you reap," is rarely taken into account when analysing one event or another, but it is strictly followed by the Masters of Wisdom. The Masters do not have the right to violate by means of supernatural powers the free will of human beings and interfere with problems created by humanity itself.

However, to the rule on non-interference in processes on Earth using supernatural powers, there are two exceptions according to which the Teachers still have the opportunity to intervene at the very last moment: firstly, when the life of the entire planet "hangs by a thread" due to human activity and secondly, when humanity itself, either as a whole or on an individual territory, calls upon the Higher Powers for help and has already applied 50% of the effort required.

As each person has their own karma, so do rulers and even countries. Thus, if during a certain historical period a ruler was prematurely removed from the throne due to some intrigue, without exhausting the time allotted to them by Karma, then the Law of Causes and Effects prescribes that in a new incarnation they must return to that same throne and serve their term. They must realize their potential, either in the positive or in the negative, so that in the end they will reap the consequences corresponding to the causes they have sown.

While the United States, as a state, is fairly young, the history of the countries of Europe and Asia is several thousand years old, and many rulers did not always die a natural death, but were killed. Therefore, some of them are now, again, in one form or another leading their countries, exhausting their karma before the start of a new cycle of human evolution.

Thus, the centuries-old history of the Romanov dynasty in Russia was filled with the most dramatic events. This resulted in the people of Russia forming the karma of regicides, which they must exhaust. After all, in 1926 the Help of Shambhala was rejected, and it is offered only when the Karma of any country allows for it. If this had been accepted, it would have helped in moving the destiny of the people in a constructive and positive direction. Now they must pay off the debt through suffering, being oppressed by those who were once overthrown by palace coups. Only Alexander I, who also met with the Count of Saint-Germain, had no karmic connection with the Romanov dynasty. When he reached the end of his term on the throne, he simulated his own death in order to spend the rest of his life in Siberia as the hermit, Saint Feodor Kuzmich.

There also exists a mystical union between Russia and Germany, where the former represents the female aspect and the latter the male. Perhaps someday an esoteric history of peoples and their rulers will be written, which will reveal the secrets of strange phenomena such as the fact that the Russians were ruled by the Germans, and which will explain the karmic connections of male and female aspects at the country level.

When the karmic denouement of the entire Romanov dynasty occurs, the Era of Divine Leaders will come to the Slavic lands, just as the Initiated Pharaohs once ruled in Ancient Egypt, bringing the spirit of newness into the life of their people. Indeed, only the peoples who over the centuries have experienced the full depth of injustice, oppression, and suffering will be able to build a true society of justice in the New World.

Helena Roerich elucidated this karmic issue even more deeply in her letters: "I wondered why Russia has such a terrible karma, for if you look at the history of all countries, many more bloody crimes were committed in other countries than in Russia. Now it is clear to me: at a time when freedom of conscience and confession were already being allowed in other countries, in Russia every disagreement with narrow dogmatism was equated with a crime against the state. It was forbidden to think, and this prohibition along with violence against the Spirit have indeed generated this terrible karma. For, truly, there is no greater crime than a crime against Spirit."[1]

Hatred is one of the most powerful energies, comparable in magnetic power to Love. Hence if a person hates someone fiercely, then by the Law of Karma in the next incarnation they can be put in the place of the one whom they so hated: yesterday's persecutor of Christians becomes persecuted for their faith today; whoever hates Muslims today will see nothing higher than the Quran tomorrow. The energy of hate can only be neutralized by love, and the Law of Karma sees to it that the balance of energies is established.

Now we can consider the consequences of wars and conflicts over the course of millennia. Millions of people hated each other, and by the Law of Karma from one life to the next they changed places in their new incarnations in order to

---

[1] Roerich, *Pis'ma*, vol. 2 (Moscow: Mezhdunarodnyy tsentr Rerikhov, 2000), p. 452.

come to love those countries, those peoples, or those religions against which they formerly shed blood. Those who took life in the past must give it in the present.

Moreover, according to the Law of Karma, if a person dies prematurely, they remain in the lowest subtle layers for precisely the amount of time that they still had to live on Earth. Until this energy of karma is exhausted, their soul cannot rise any higher. Therefore, suicide is one of the gravest sins. Thus, where from time to time rivers of blood were shed, huge numbers of people who died prematurely as a result of murder hang in the near-Earth space for centuries, and there these hundreds of thousands and millions of undead souls continue to fight with each other, since this is all they know.

Using the example of the medieval Inquisition, Helena Roerich explained: "The Inquisition, forcibly interrupting the lives of millions of its victims, gave rise to a terrible calamity of possession. For, from the Teaching, we know that spirits who are plunged into the Subtle World before the expiration of the normal term of their life, yearn to touch the vital earthly power through any vehicle available to them. They are still full of the unexhausted reserve of the magnetic force that binds them to Earth, often being unable to perceive currents of higher frequency due to the low level of development of their consciousness. Both malice and revenge drew these victims to their executioners, and through possession, they forced them to commit even greater crimes, even to end their own life in suicide, in order to absorb and enjoy the emanations of their blood, giving them, albeit for a short time, the illusion of life."[1]

This is why one of the goals of the dark forces throughout the history of humanity has been the formation of totalitarian regimes in various territories based on mass murders and the suppression of free will. The means of possession enabled them

---

[1] Roerich, *Pis'ma*, vol. 2, p. 279.

to extend their power even to the rulers and inhabitants of non-participating countries.

"One can often observe how those possessed act contrary to common sense, only to vomit evil. It is important that we understand just how numerous are the atrocities committed to appease an invisible villain. People called them demons, but one may simply call them scum. It cannot be assumed that possession requires a powerful demon. Every earthly criminal undoubtedly strives to become a possessor and thereby feed their enduring hatred. ... Many historical events have taken place under the influence of possession — let us not forget this."[1]

"Many countries are ruled by individuals who are mad in the full sense of the word. The manifestation of mass possession was not something that occurred previously; it is incomprehensible that scientists have not paid attention to what is such a disaster! People create millions of murders. Does it really not occur to anyone that this is a hotbed of possession?"[2]

Thus, these invisible possessors, demanding food in the form of energy or blood, attach themselves to those who are physically incarnate and feed on their energy, and it does not matter who it is: an ordinary person or the ruler of an entire country. They instil in people thoughts of murder or suicide, which their victims assume to be their own and often carry out. Terrorist attacks, shootings in educational establishments, serial killings, bloody conflicts — all are the consequence of possession. After all, this is the 21st century, not the Middle Ages, when any problem was solved through violence. Possession tends to take hold of people at a low level of spiritual development, since the aura of a spiritual and loving person forms a special protective net that scorches dark entities.

---

[1] Roerich, *Agni Yoga s kommentariyami*, vol. 2, p. 1107.
[2] Roerich, *Agni Yoga s kommentariyami*, vol. 2, p. 244.

When a sufficient number of such entities are gathered, these "armies" are skilfully used by the evil forces, and if there are voluntary or involuntary executors of their "strategies" on the physical plane, then it is as if invisible near-Earth battles "break through" and find their reflection in the earthly world. In this way the "soldiers" of the lowest layers of the Subtle Plane begin to use the hands of the physically incarnate to continue to kill and fight, multiplying evil and enveloping as many territories of the planet as possible. Syria and Ukraine are examples of this, and earlier, "breakthroughs" of the battles from the Subtle World were reflected in Chechnya, Nagorno-Karabakh, the Caucasus, Transnistria, the former republics of Yugoslavia, and so on. The two world wars also represented a reflection of what was happening on the Subtle Plane.

Let us quote the Great Lord of Shambhala: "We are all saddened by the savagery of humanity. The wildest manifestation of free will is war. People do not want to think about the kind of currents they evoke or the consequences of mass murder! The most ancient Precepts correctly pointed out that whoever takes up the sword will perish by the sword.

"The karma of the attacker differs from that of the defender. It can be shown to what extent all attackers are subjected to the gravest consequences, and in the Subtle World, too, their situation is not easy. People usually take comfort in the idea that great conquerors do not feel their karma during their earthly lives. But karma does not manifest itself immediately. It approaches everyone in a special way. In the end, is life not continuous? The wise perceive their earthly lives as the pearls of a single necklace.

"Now let us remind the attackers that they burden their karma not only by killing, but also by clogging the atmosphere, which is something that occurs in every war. Such poisoning of the Earth and other spheres remains for a long time.

"You, invaders of the lands of your neighbours, has no one ever told you what the consequences of your fratricide will be?

"Our Abode has witnessed many wars. We can tell you to what extent such evil increases in the most unexpected forms. People know that shots cause rain, but will poisonous gases not evoke the most terrible phenomena? Thus, you can imagine how sorrowful We are upon seeing the wildest manifestation of your free will. However, such will was bestowed upon you as a supreme gift."[1]

The point of the last paragraph can be illustrated with specific examples for our clearer understanding of the consequences of wars unleashed by earthly rulers at the instigation of dark forces.

In 1996, a Russian researcher discovered that the negative energy of a large number of people causes fluctuations in Earth's magnetic field. In a certain number of days after such noticeable impulses, earthquakes with a force of at least 6 points on the Richter scale occur in quake-prone areas, and natural disasters may occur in other parts of the globe: hurricanes, typhoons, floods, tornadoes, etc.[2]

Now let us look at the years 1939, 1999, and 2023: the strongest earthquakes shook Turkey, taking tens of thousands of lives. But what else do these dates have in common?

1939 — the German invasion of Poland and the beginning of the Second World War; 1999 — the unauthorized bombing of Yugoslavia; 2023 — Russia's unjustified war against Ukraine, when in November–December 2022, Russians deliberately attacked infrastructure facilities leaving millions of Ukrainians without electricity and water. In all three cases, there was a

---

[1] Roerich, *Agni Yoga s kommentariyami*, vol. 2, pp. 799–800.

[2] Valeriy Balurin, "Energiya vozmushcheniya bol'shogo kolichestva lyudey vyzyvayet kolebaniya magnitnogo polya Zemli" [The indignation energy of a large number of people causes fluctuations in the Earth's magnetic field], *Anomaliya*, https://ufonews.su/text5/609.htm.

massive release of negative emotion and thought from millions of people on the European continent. And in the third case, the war against Ukraine was reflected in strong earthquakes in other parts of the planet in 2022: Japan, Mexico, and Italy. In general, if scientists were to mark resonant negative events over many years on a map of the world, and then compare these with the geographical location of natural disasters, they would discover a striking pattern and interconnectedness.

Scientists at the HeartMath Institute in the United States have reached the conclusion that each heart is capable of affecting Earth's electromagnetic field, the information carrier for all living beings; accordingly, a collective of hearts is able to influence all life on the planet, both positively and negatively.[1]

Prior to this, beginning in 1978, a number of scientific experiments were conducted in the United States that confirmed the fact that if a few thousand people meditate for a length of time with the aim of having a positive impact on a certain territory, the result will be statistically measurable: the number of crimes, acts of violence, and death rate will decrease.[2] In 1993, it was scientifically determined that a meditating group of 2,500 people could influence 1.5 million.[3] So what then might be the impact of the tens of millions of people involved in a war?

Indeed, the collective will of humanity is able to both save the planet and explode it, and the forces of darkness are working especially hard in the direction of the latter. However, it

---

[1] Rollin McCraty, *Science of the Heart, Volume 2*, (Boulder Creek, CA: HeartMath Institute, 2015), p. 89.

[2] Guy Hatchard et al, "Maharishi Effect: A Model for Social Improvement. Time Series Analysis of a Phase Transition to Reduced Crime in Merseyside Metropolitan Area," *Psychology, Crime & Law*, vol. 2 (1996), pp. 165–174.

[3] John Hagelin et al, "Results of the National Demonstration Project to Reduce Violent Crime and Improve Governmental Effectiveness in Washington, D.C.," *Social Indicators Research*, vol. 47 (June 1999), pp. 153–201.

should be said outright that the Great Teachers will not allow the destruction of the planet to take place; however, the same cannot be said of particular countries and continents, where everything depends solely on the free will of the people inhabiting them.

So, with just a few examples, we can see how we are all interconnected and how the destinies of countries change when they accept, even partially, guidance from the Secret Government of Shambhala. And we can also see the far-reaching consequences of the complete rejection of the outstretched Hand of Help that are reaped not only by those countries that refuse it, but by those, too, that are seemingly uninvolved.

The advice that was expressed in written form is but a small fraction of what might have been given to the leaders of certain countries. Nonetheless, the main guidance always takes place on the invisible plane: the leaders' souls are inspired by creative ideas and solutions as seemingly insoluble problems arise.

For example, the Lord of Shambhala had telepathic conversations with President Roosevelt to help him resolve the issues that confronted him as head of state.[1] The President did not know anything about the Himalayan Brotherhood, but the most important thing was that he "lived from his heart"[2] and genuinely wanted to do good for his people, although "half measures impeded him."[3]

Of course, after receiving such "rich experience" of rejection, the Masters of Wisdom no longer personally turn towards governments, unless they themselves, caring for the good of their peoples, take certain steps towards the Teachers of Humanity.

---

[1] See Roerich, *Zapisi Ucheniya Zhivoy Etiki*, vol. 13 (Wismar, 2011), p. 232.
[2] Roerich, *Zapisi Ucheniya Zhivoy Etiki*, vol. 13, p. 337.
[3] Roerich, *Zapisi Ucheniya Zhivoy Etiki*, vol. 13, p. 338.

And if the leaders of certain countries had accepted the Higher Assistance at the time it was offered, then now the question on the agenda would have been how to unite the European Union, the United States of both Americas, and the Union of the East into a single whole. Of course, if people had been able to put into practice at least a small portion of the Advice emanating from the Highest Sources, we would now be just a step away from the true Golden Age — the era of happiness, peace, and prosperity, forever forgetting the grief and misfortune that we witness in our current reality.

"Urusvati can testify to the healing vibrations sent by Us. Their rhythms are diverse. Not everyone is able to discern them. Some will assume them to be an earthquake; some will suspect a bout of fever; some will attribute it all to their own excitement; but most people will think that it was just in their imagination. Nevertheless, Our healing care is often felt on different continents. People receive help and experience unexpected recovery, but they do not understand where the help originated. We are not talking about gratitude as We do not need it. However, conscious acceptance of help intensifies its beneficial effect. Every denial and case of mockery paralyses even strong vibrations. We rush to help. We hasten to bring good, but how often are We welcomed?

"The ignorant assert that it is We who incite revolutions and discord. But actually We have many times attempted to prevent and avert murders and destruction. Brother Rakoczy personally fulfilled the highest measure of love for humanity and was rejected by those for whom He cared. The records remained, now widely known, yet some liars still call Him the father of the French Revolution.

"Likewise, people fail to understand Our appeal to Queen Victoria, and yet history itself has demonstrated how right We were. Our warning was rejected. But Our duty is to warn peoples. Our warning to Moscow was also not understood. It will be some time before people come to remember this and compare it with their reality. We could cite many historical facts from the life of different countries. We could recall Napoleon, and the appearance of the Counsellor of the American Constitution, the manifestation in Sweden, and the indication concerning Spain.

"Let people remember that it has been ten years since the destruction of Spain [in the Civil War] was indicated. The sign of salvation was given, but, as is customary, it was not accepted. Everywhere We rush to help. And We rejoice when it is accepted. We are sad to see the kind of fate that peoples prefer."[1]

Helena Roerich wrote: "America and Russia are the countries of the future. Tests, if they are passed with honour, will only help the flourishing."[2] Similarly, in his prophecies, Edgar Cayce pointed out the importance of friendship between Russia and America for the salvation of the world: "In Russia there comes the hope of the world, not as that sometimes termed of the Communistic, of the Bolshevistic; no. But freedom, freedom! that each man will live for his fellow man! The principle has been born. It will take years for it to be crystallized, but out of Russia comes again the hope of the world. Guided by what? That friendship with the nation that hath even set on its present monetary unit 'In God We Trust.'"[3] He also said that this hope depended on the spiritual development of Russia: "On Russia's religious development will come the greater hope of the world."[4] However, this will not happen until "there is

---

[1] Roerich, *Agni Yoga s kommentariyami*, vol. 2, p. 737.

[2] Roerich, *Pis'ma*, vol. 5 (Moscow: Mezhdunarodnyy tsentr Rerikhov, 2003), p. 99.

[3] Edgar Cayce, *The Complete Edgar Cayce Readings* (Virginia Beach, VA: A.R.E. Press, 2006), CD-ROM, Reading 3976–29.

[4] Cayce, Reading 3976–10.

freedom of speech, and the right to worship according to the dictates of conscience."[1]

It is no coincidence that Helena Blavatsky, who became the first woman from the Russian Empire to take US citizenship, and the Roerich family were sent from the Slavic lands to America in order to accomplish the mission assigned by Shambhala. Blavatsky needed to spread Theosophy, or Divine Wisdom, and the Roerichs needed to imbue the art and culture of modern America with spirituality. Nonetheless, during the lifetime of Blavatsky and the Roerichs, their works could not be freely published in their own homeland.

According to many other prophecies and predictions in both the West and the East, the Slavs, by virtue of their astrological association with the sign of Aquarius and the New Age, are destined to play a key role in the evolution of humanity on Earth through the creation of a new spiritual pattern of life for the whole world. Therefore, all the blows that the darkness can possibly muster are vehemently directed at the Slavic lands in order to prevent this from happening, acting from within to incite strife for contrived reasons.

In Helena Roerich's recently published notebooks, there is an interesting entry: "Ukraine preserves the core of the best Rus' people, and Kyiv bore the name Mother of Rus' Cities. ... Ukraine is the original Rus.'"[2]

Hence one may realize why for centuries the freedom-loving people of Ukraine was suppressed by force and repression, driving it into slavery and banning its language and culture. But the most "inventive" in this dark matter was Stalin, who, in addition to mass arrests and shootings, for the first time in the world, in 1932–1933 organized an artificial

---

[1] Cayce, Reading 3976-19.

[2] Helena Roerich, "Zapisi besed s Uchitelem (mashinopis')" [Records of conversations with the Master (typescript)], 04.03.1953–15.08.1953, fol. 19, Roerich Museum, Moscow.

famine, which took the lives of millions of Ukrainians, in order to suppress and tame the recalcitrant nation.

In this regard, it is worth mentioning another aspect that explains why conflicts on the planet occur in certain places over the centuries. On Earth there are places of power called *Points of Life*. Since ancient times, the Initiates have built temples at these sites and there embedded special energy magnets that are associated with certain constellations or individual celestial bodies. These magnets receive their currents and project them onto entrusted territories, which can sometimes be quite far on the geographical map from the Points themselves. The most prominent examples are the Pyramids in Egypt associated with Orion, and Stonehenge in the United Kingdom, with Sirius.

Points of Life serve as collectors and accumulators of special power, which purifies and saturates the space around them with positive and creative energy. Also, their energy activity is able to harmonize underground fire, which, due to the imperfect low-frequency thinking of humanity, threatens to break out and result in large-scale natural disasters. In some cases, Points of Life are designed to prevent fratricidal wars.

In total, there are twelve main Points of Life scattered around the world. From time to time they might change location depending on Cosmic and spatial conditions. Thus, these magnets must work as a single coordinated organism.

Each main Point is duodecimal in essence — that is, there are 144 magnets in total, which were laid all over the Earth by the Great Initiates according to the laws of sacred geometry, both on the dense plane and on the Subtle Plane. The failure of one Point can disrupt the energetic harmony of the entire entrusted territory and impede the circulation of energies with the Fiery Heart of the planet — Shambhala.

However, magnets of another kind should be noted, too — those that are composed of a collection of artifacts, ancient manuscripts, and works of art that were created or belonged to the Initiates of all times and ages, since they have been imbued with their powerful energy. In this way, Points of Life appear as certain museums and libraries around the world: the Louvre Museum, the Egyptian Museum, the British Museum, and others.

Near and in opposition to Points of Life, the forces of darkness always attempt to form their own Points of Death in order to disturb the energy balance of the planet. Points of Death grow at the expense of bloody emanations, and, therefore, they constantly demand food mixed on a conflict basis from a simple negative attitude towards someone to the point of war. The minions of darkness thereby try to burden the vibrational frequency of the magnets embedded in Points of Life in an attempt to "incline" their Power to the side of darkness so as to employ it for their own vile purposes.

For example, in Israel, all the holy sites associated with Christ are Points of Life. But in order to drown out their Power, there is the Israeli–Palestinian conflict. By the same analogy, the India–Pakistan conflict, because there are many places in India associated with the Masters. A long time ago, the mountains of Ethiopia concealed an ancient female Sanctuary, and so as to exterminate its positive energy, there was one of the most brutal civil wars in Africa, the echoes of which also occurred in 2020–2022. Many other analogies may be cited throughout history.

If we look at the map, we may note that conflicts mostly have taken place near mountain ranges — natural Points of Life: the Alps, the Caucasus, the Carpathians, the Himalayas, and so on. This is due to the fact that mountains receive high cosmic energies and also preserve a special conglomerate of Fires, on which the movement of new currents in the world depends. Certain mountain ranges, not only the Himalayas, conceal the Abodes of Shambhala, which intensify these Points of Life. Therefore, by instigating conflicts of various kinds from the Subtle Plane, evil forces try to prevent the flow of currents and to change the positive formulas of these energies to negative ones. After all, the emanations of blood very quickly alter the energy formula at the level of the physical plane, and this results in a destructive energy that goes out into the world.

Each place and each magnet laid has its own time for awakening, and as soon as this time approaches, so the forces of darkness try to gain a foothold at one point or another, many centuries in advance. For example, the time of the awakening of the Caucasus, whose ancient civilization was associated with the Initiates of Egypt, came at the end of the 20th century — this is why such serious problems have arisen in this region from century to century, and even in the current, 21st century.

But in the case of the Slavic lands, whose high spiritual purpose has been known since antiquity, it is interesting to note the "multipass" strategy of the forces of darkness.

It has already been said above that King Solomon possessed a fragment of the mystical Chintamani Stone. King Solomon was an Initiate, and, therefore, could see and know much deeper than ordinary rulers. In the 10th century BCE, he laid a magnet in the foundation of his Temple in Jerusalem. He also founded the city of Palmyra, which is located on the territory of modern-day Syria, where he laid a special stone. Despite the fact that many centuries have passed since then and that these places have suffered destruction, the magnets still exist. However, the purpose of these two Points of Life was to receive rays from Sirius and project them onto the Slavic lands when the magnets were to be revived at the end of the 20th century.

Nevertheless, within just a few years, a new round of Arab–Israeli conflicts began, with thousands of victims. Then, in 2011, a civil war broke out in Syria. And then its territory was seized by the so-called "Islamic State," which was a pure progeny of the dark forces, and had nothing to do with Islam.

The lands of Syria were literally drowned in blood, while the effective activity of Points of Life requires a peaceful sky and prayerful service. And it was no coincidence that the terrorists destroyed the ancient temples of Palmyra and other sites of cultural heritage in the region. We may also recall how in 2001, the same fanatics demolished ancient statues in Afghanistan that were created by the hands of the Initiates long before they were remade into Buddha statues, testifying to the fact that human civilization was much older than is commonly believed.

As mentioned previously, one of the tasks of Points of Life is to prevent fratricidal war, since their energies are able to bring harmony to places where discord is brewing. After shedding much blood near the magnets laid by King Solomon, the dark forces managed to disrupt the circulation of energies between these sites and the Slavic lands. The consequences were not long in coming — the first serious clash between the Russian Federation and Ukraine began in 2014.

It is also interesting to note that, 2400 years ago, an Initiate laid a sacred stone imbued with the Chintamani currents in a grotto in the Crimea on the Black Sea coast. Its awakening time came in 2015. Looking at the events not only of 2014, but also in history as a whole, we can see all the "preparatory work" of the dark forces, and how many bloody battles for the Crimea were waged from one century to the next, preventing the lower layers of the Subtle World from being cleansed of the masses of those whose lives were taken prematurely.

Therefore, any battle for the Crimea is very dangerous and risky from this point of view, since it is capable of triggering all layers of the battles in the lowest astral planes, which can then "break through" into our physical world and result in the most severe slaughter involving many countries, forming a giant deadly funnel.

The lands of Ukraine, like those of Russia, are blessed with Points of Life. Some became active from 1999 onwards, and those that were already active have been transferred to a new energetic level.

As for Russia, in connection with the aforementioned names of Saint Sergius of Radonezh and Alexander I, it is worth noting the Points of Life founded by them. In the 14th century, while still a youth, Sergius of Radonezh received from a mysterious stranger a magnet-stone which he was tasked with laying in the foundations of a holy site, now known as the Trinity Lavra of Saint Sergius. And in 1817, King Alexander I, who was also an Initiate, laid a magnet in the foundations of the Cathedral of Christ the Saviour in Moscow. In 1931, the cathedral was destroyed by order of the Soviet government, but was rebuilt in 1999. Of course, there are many other Points in Russia aside from these. But let us move on to the main Points in Ukraine.

In the 11th century, the Grand Prince of Kyiv, Yaroslav the Wise, laid a mystical stone in the foundations of the Saint Sophia Cathedral — a temple dedicated to the Power and Supreme Wisdom of God. It was revived in 1999. Since then, at a certain time, three times a day, it emits a host of rays, which can be registered using special devices. These rays of Love-Wisdom spread in concentric circles and cover not only the whole of Ukraine, but also portions of all neighbouring countries. Thus, the souls of Ukrainians among all Slavic peoples became pioneers in the field of receiving new energies of Love-Wisdom to the extent of their capacity, just as Christianity once spread from here to all the Slavic lands. These energies are projected onto human hearts, because the future belongs to the heart alone. For this reason, the Temple of Sophia has been threatened with complete destruction on more than one occasion: in the Soviet 1930s, during the Second World War, and in 2022.¹

The Pochaev Lavra in Western Ukraine may also be mentioned. The main portal of one of its cathedrals is decorated with a mosaic of Nicholas Roerich. This Point of Life is interconnected with the sacred place of the confluence of three rivers in India, the Sangam. In addition, in Eastern Ukraine there are Points of Life associated with future humanity. They have not yet awakened, but the forces of evil are already trying to settle nearby with the goal of suffocating them.

One of these is the Svyatogorsk Lavra where the magnet was laid by an Initiate of the Theban Sanctuary. It started pulsing in 1999. This Point of Life, along with Luxor in Egypt and the Abode in the Himalayas, was kept from underground movements by the former Lord of Shambhala, Mahatma Serapis. On the way to Mariupol ("the city of Mary"), there is another Point connected with future humanity, although still in a dormant state, awaiting its time. Hence, the shelling of the Lavra in 2022 was not at all accidental, nor was the fact that the city of Mary by the sea was ruthlessly and almost completely destroyed creating thousands of victims — news that shocked the entire civilized world.

Thus, by analysing Points of Life in a context that goes beyond geographic and political boundaries, one may understand

---

[1] See Oleg Shama, "Sofiya spasennaya. Kak drevneyshiy khram Ukrainy yedva ne pogib ot sovetskikh vlastey, spetssluzhb i vremeni" [Sophia saved. How the oldest temple in Ukraine almost perished at the hands of Soviet power, the intelligence agency, and time], *Novoye Vremya*, https://nv.ua/kyiv/sofiya-kievskaya-kak-drevneyshiy-sobor-chut-ne-pogib-iz-za-sovetov-specsluzhb-i-vremeni-2514500.html; Vladimir Kostyrin, "Rossiyskiye okkupanty planirovali unichtozhit' Sofiyu Kiyevskuyu: kak oberegali ukrainskuyu svyatynyu" [Russian invaders planned to destroy Sophia of Kyiv: how the Ukrainian shrine was protected], *RBK-Ukraina*, https://www.rbc.ua/ukr/styler/rosiyski-okupanti-planuvali-znishchiti-sofiyu-1667314444.html.

the deeper causes and true motives of the extremely negative events taking place in the Slavic lands, and by analogy, in other territories, without being deceived by the "good intentions" that supposedly justify the strangulation of various sacred magnets. Those who truly carry the Light will never drown it out or desecrate what is holy. Indeed, when there is the sincere desire to avoid all conflict and establish real peace, then there will always be ways and wise decisions inspired from Above.

The difference between the wars that took place centuries ago and the wars of today is that now all the Points of Life and Forces of Light are strained to the limit trying to keep the planet from exploding due to the fact that the entire Solar System is passing through an energetically dangerous zone in the Cosmos. And at this most crucial time, despite all the warnings issued both by Nature and the Masters of Wisdom, humanity still cannot calm down, come to its senses, and ponder what it is doing and to what this might lead.

Just as a person has energy centres, chakras, on the subtle plane, so too does planet Earth. And it has long been no secret that the Slavic lands represent the Heart. This is why between these lands and Shambhala, which represents the Fiery Heart, there is an invisible connection, just as in the sevenfold human structure there is a connection between the physical, subtle, and fiery hearts. No matter how healthy other organs are, the health of the entire organism depends on the heart. If it falls sick, the whole body suffers. So what will the darkness target throughout history? It is obvious that it will strike right to the heart, to its core, in order not only to cut short the spiritual mission entrusted to the Slavs as a whole, but also to more swiftly disable the entire body, thereby disturbing the planetary balance. This imbalance threatens the peril of all that exists — and this is exactly what the forces of evil want.

In this connection, it is interesting to recall the second secret of the Virgin Mary, who appeared to children in the city of Fátima, Portugal, in 1917 — a phenomenon which was recognized as a genuine miracle. It went as follows: "If my requests are heeded, Russia will be converted, and there will be peace; if not, she will spread her errors throughout the world, causing wars and persecutions of the Church."[1] In order to turn the USSR to spirituality and the right construction of society, an attempt was made by the Roerichs to warn its government in 1926, but this was rejected, and all that the Virgin Mary warned of consequently followed.

Famous American mystic and astrologer Max Heindel predicted: "When ... the Sun ... shall have entered the sign Aquarius, the Russian people and the Slav Races in general will reach a degree of spiritual development which will advance them far beyond their present condition. ... The Slavic civilization will be ... great and joyful ... for it is being born of deep sorrow and untold suffering, and the law of Compensation will bring the opposite in due time."[2]

Between the Slavic and American lands there is an energetic connection, similar to a circulatory system on which depends the vitality of not only the peoples inhabiting these territories, but also the health of the planet as a whole. If "thrombosis" occurs in one of the "arteries" due to the accumulation of negative energy, then the disease will threaten the entire body. That is why Mahatma Morya especially emphasized the need for friendship between Russia and America, which would be capable of preventing impending natural disasters of catastrophic proportions: "The Salvation of the World depends on America's friendly attitude towards Russia, but

---

[1] Lucia Santos, *Fatima in Lucia's Own Words*, vol. 1 (Fátima, Portugal: Secretariado Dos Pastorinhos, 2007), p.124.

[2] Max Heindel, *The Rosicrucian Cosmo-Conception* (Ocean Park, CA: Rosicrucian Fellowship, 1911), pp. 305–306.

this is impossible due to the state of mind of those in these countries and their rulers."[1]

Edgar Cayce described with immense accuracy the places and timing of the cataclysms that should have changed the geographical map almost beyond recognition. We may also recall the warning of Helena Blavatsky that the 20th century "may even be the last of its name,"[2] as well as that of Helena Roerich: "The most dangerous moment for our planet will come at the end of this century. Specifically, the planet will experience the question — to be or not to be?"[3]

At the cost of the Great Sacrifice of the Teachers, the main catastrophe, which could have greatly affected both America and Europe as a result of the movements of underground fire, "has been postponed for one century — perhaps, even, for two."[4] But if humanity does not come to its senses and does not jointly ponder how to protect its home from destruction, then it could occur as early as in this 21st century.

From the very beginning, the Great Teachers have paid much attention to America, and for the purpose of awakening its uniquely formed people to spirituality, it has been given more than any other country. And although the attempts of the Masters of Wisdom were accompanied by terrible betrayals, which led to their deep sense of disappointment in the middle of the 20th century, no one cancelled the special mission entrusted to the American people. For they still should take a

---

[1] Helena Roerich, "Zapisi besed s Uchitelem (kosmicheskoye sotrudnichestvo)" [Records of conversations with the Master (cosmic cooperation)], 23.03.1950–23.05.1950, fol. 41, Roerich Museum, Moscow.

[2] H. P. Blavatsky, "The Esoteric Character of the Gospels," *Collected Writings*, vol. 8 (Wheaton, IL: Theosophical Publishing House, 1966), p. 205.

[3] Roerich, *Pis'ma*, vol. 6, p. 133.

[4] Helena Roerich, "Zapisi besed s Uchitelem (mashinopis')" [Records of conversations with the Master (typescript)], 04.03.1953–15.08.1953, fol. 60, Roerich Museum, Moscow.

giant step from materiality to spirituality, becoming purer and more heart-centred.

Hence this book is now more relevant than ever. It was compiled by Helena Roerich in 1933 from conversations with Mahatma Morya, the Lord of Shambhala, and was entitled *Guidance for the Leader*. It was intended for a new generation of individuals called to become leaders, who see the meaning of their existence in serving humanity in all spheres of life. The book contains much advice relating to parenting, education, economics, and many other issues. Particular attention is paid to the principles that enlightened leaders should follow in their internal personal and external public life. And although it is addressed to persons vested in power, the spiritual principles outlined in these pages can be applied by anyone in daily life. After all, you do not have to occupy a high position in order to start changing the world for the better.

The Master asked Helena Roerich to start compiling the book *Guidance for the Leader* on 25 June 1933.[1] The introductory word was given on 24 March of the same year. At that time, Roerich was also gathering historical facts about the Ambassadors of Light for a letter to America, which were supplemented by the Teacher.

On 1 June, she sent this letter to her American colleagues. It almost entirely repeated her first letter to Roosevelt in the following year. One of her colleagues was a friend of Henry Wallace, the US Secretary of Agriculture at the time. It is for him that these historical facts were intended, so as to prepare the ground with Roosevelt. Here follow excerpts from it, not included in further correspondence with the President:

"Dear ones, in addition to the most interesting biblical prophecy sent to us by Maurice, I want to inform you that I, too, am now reading a wonderful document compiled on the

---

[1] See Roerich, *Zapisi Ucheniya Zhivoy Etiki*, vol. 13, p. 140.

basis of attested historical data. It has gathered turning points in the history of many countries and peoples and shows the reasons, in most cases hidden from wide publicity, but which served to their flourish or fall. And invariably these causes consisted in accepting or rejecting the advice or warnings that came to them in the most unexpected and varied form, and always, as the Author points out, these counsels came from the Source of Good, for the corresponding consequences were and are vivid witnesses to this. I will give you just a few examples, closer to our time.

"So, from Chinese sources, we see that during the time of Genghis Khan there was an Elder of the Mountain, who gave him advice that led to such a flourishing of his reign. In the place cited, there is a narration of the following episode: when ambassadors from the Elder of the Mountain were received by Genghis Khan, the casket they brought contained a golden chalice and many covers of various colours and bore this inscription: 'Drink from one chalice, but cover yourself with the robes of all peoples.' Thus were indicated the Hierarchy and tolerance, as befits a leader. At the same time, the Author provides noteworthy comments: 'The Leader will not have a predilection for nations, for during creation, workers may be unexpected. Rulers usually err when they limit themselves to sympathetic prejudice. The creator of a planet cannot make it only in gold or iron; instead he brings all the elements to the ratio. What is new will not be old.' …

"Thus, we can see warnings and advice of great importance throughout history. But what is most interesting about this book is that the Author, by all indications of our time, asserts that America has now approached a milestone, or turning point, in her history. And he cites an old prophecy that under Roosevelt there will be big changes. 'America can achieve great significance and peaceful prosperity. Counsel is ready for America, and it is good for her to accept it. But she must receive the ambassador and show respect, for otherwise there are many examples of the terrible consequences of rejections.'

"So, from this book we see that Roosevelt's rule can be unprecedentedly brilliant, but may also end like Hoover's if the Counsel is rejected, and this is indeed what happened. Will Roosevelt really turn out to be a spirit less than Washington? It is interesting to note that many applied this prophecy about Roosevelt to the first president of this name, and only now it is clear from certain small details that it referred to the present one.

"Then the Author of this wonderful historical document draws attention to the fact that the counsels of this Benevolent Source are always easy to implement. They never belittle the country to which the advice is given. Much attention is given to legends about Prester John, and in several countries his wonderful messages to the heads of countries and the Church (Popes of Rome) are preserved. Most of these documents date back to the 12th and 13th centuries. However, as history shows, the good advice contained in these letters was usually not accepted. Several embassies are indicated, which were dispatched to this Prester John in Central Asia, to his supposed place of residence. But since the purpose of the embassy was insincere, they could not reach it. Of course, you have no doubt Who this Prester John was.

"I end the excerpts of these examples with the final prophecy taken by the Author from ancient Jewish writings: 'The people of Amos can come to a worthy decision only by the command of the White Mountain, otherwise I see many a grievous omen. I clearly see that there can be only one solution, and no one and nothing will change this inevitable world construction.' Such amazing documents, aren't they, my dear ones? And one should treat them with all care and caution, so that America will not suffer the fate of countries that have rejected the good Counsel!

"Modrochka[1] wrote that her friend Wallace is very fond of collecting prophecies; therefore, of course, she must see him and personally convey or read to him the 'extracts' I have given. If I were the Ruler, I would accept such a message as the forerunner of a historic day for America, and would apply every effort, all aspiration, so as not to bypass the Ambassador of Good, but to hear him out and fulfil as accurately as possible all of his Counsels. Undoubtedly, he will appear, for we see how historical examples repeat themselves. But one needs to be able to recognize him. Yes, in all these documents one is able to see how countries can harm themselves by going against the Hierarchy of Light!"[2]

Before sending this letter, the Great Lord of Shambhala said on 24 May 1933:

"Now it is up to them whether to succeed. Hoover has already set an example of how unhelpful it is to reject My Advice. So now Roosevelt has the opportunity to assist the glory of America by accepting My Command. If he knew what Moscow lost by not accepting My Command, perhaps he would hasten to heed My Will. Let him not say that he did not know when Wallace told him about Fuyama.[3] Being busy is no excuse; the leader should draw on heart-based wisdom and not be inclined to turn a deaf ear. So before your eyes there are already a number of examples of disobedience to My Command, and the destiny of the country depends on a deaf ear."[4]

In total, no more than ten copies of the typewritten manuscript of *Guidance for the Leader* were produced. One of these was taken by Nicholas Roerich to the United States in 1934 to be presented as a gift to President Roosevelt through Henry

---

[1] Frances Ruth Grant.
[2] Roerich, *Pis'ma*, vol. 1 (Moscow: Mezhdunarodnyy tsentr Rerikhov, 1999), pp. 392–394.
[3] Nicholas Roerich's spiritual name.
[4] Roerich, *Zapisi Ucheniya Zhivoy Etiki*, vol. 13, pp. 86–87.

Wallace, as the former held Roerich and his cultural initiatives in high esteem, while the President's mother, Sarah, was an admirer of his work.

So, in 1935, the so-called Roerich Pact (the Treaty on the Protection of Artistic and Scientific Institutions and Historic Monuments) was signed in Washington, and became the first international treaty specifically dedicated to the protection of cultural property. Thanks to his international cultural activities, Nicholas Roerich was nominated three times for the Nobel Peace Prize: in 1929, 1932, and 1935. Later, based on the Roerich Pact, there followed the signing of the Hague Convention for the Protection of Cultural Property in the Event of Armed Conflict.

In past lifetimes, the hand of Nicholas Roerich's spirit had already created masterpieces of painting, such as the *Mona Lisa* and the *Last Supper*. In all Leonardo da Vinci's works there are encrypted messages: in colours, composition, graphics, etc. There are twelve keys to deciphering the still unsolved Da Vinci Code. And in the 20th century, the entire Hierarchy of Light assisted Nicholas Roerich in painting his pictures. So, the four Greatest Spirits, who took upon themselves the burden of guiding humanity, who studied the sound of energies and human vibrations (emotional, mental, sound, etc.), participated in the creation of the Mystery of Colour in Roerich's paintings. Because Colour is Light, Light is Sound, and vice versa. Colour, Light, and Sound represent a single triad, three aspects, which are able to create worlds.

It is no longer a secret that colour has a great influence on a person. Thus, the colours contained in Roerich's paintings, radiating an invisible and inaudible sound, directly affect the higher energy centres (chakras) of any person and are designed to awaken creative abilities. Therefore, it is not at all accidental that some people experience healing upon viewing his paintings in person, while others begin to write or draw.

When the Roerich family were living in America, the doctors of a certain clinic conducted an experiment: they took under their supervision two wards of patients experiencing the same diseases of the same degree of severity. The doctors hung Nicholas Roerich's paintings in one ward and not the other. As a result, the patients in the ward with the paintings recovered on average three times faster than those in the other ward. It was Mahatma Morya who additionally endowed them with this healing effect: "I want to give the gift of healing illnesses to Roerich's paintings. … The presence of his painting is similar to a disinfection. In case of a dangerous illness, immerse your eyes in the painting intently and for a long time."[1]

There are even scientific studies proving that Roerich's paintings radiate a powerful energy and that they are able to increase the intensity of heart luminosity in those who contemplate them.[2]

Thus, these paintings along with other sacred objects exhibited at the Nicholas Roerich Museum in New York City serve as a special Point of Life and a source of powerful positive energy that keeps and protects not only the city itself, but also a significant portion of the United States.

On 15 September 1934, Mahatma Morya told Helena Roerich that she could start to think over her letter to Roosevelt.[3] Initially, she intended to pass it through Henry Wallace, but in the end it was entrusted to Louis Horch.

After receiving this historic message on 28 October, Roosevelt showed a special and deep interest in Helena Roerich and from that time onwards awaited her replies. His first

---

[1] Roerich, *Zapisi Ucheniya Zhivoy Etiki*, vol. 3 (Moscow, 2008), p. 76.
[2] M. G. Starchenko et al, "Ob energetike kartin N. K. Rerikha" [On the energy of Nicholas Roerich's paintings], *Novaya Epokha*, Issue 23 (1999), http://www.newepoch.ru/journals/23/energy_painting.html.
[3] See Roerich, *Zapisi Ucheniya Zhivoy Etiki*, vol. 14 (Wismar, 2012), p. 314.

questions, which were always transmitted orally and not in writing, were conveyed to Roerich on 10 November.

However, over time, Louis Horch along with his wife Nettie, who were well received in the White House and had been colleagues of the Roerichs for 14 years, still could not resist the temptation to present their personal desire to enrich themselves in the form of advice coming from Shambhala. When they were caught in this dishonest act, they resorted to besmirching the name of the Roerichs in America and before President Roosevelt.

This betrayal and slander inflicted an irreparable blow on the reputation and affairs of the Roerichs in the United States, just as previously Helena Blavatsky was betrayed by the Coulombs in order to fabricate evidence for the accusatory report of the Society for Psychical Research, which only a hundred years later, in 1986, came to the conclusion that Blavatsky "was unjustly condemned."[1] Alas, history tends to repeat itself, and these examples show how strong is the influence of the dark forces, who always try to discredit the activities of the Messengers of Shambhala.

In 1937, at the request of Helena Roerich, *Guidance for the Leader* was printed in Riga, Latvia, with a run of just fifty copies, each being numbered. In her letters, she emphasizes that without her permission, no one should copy or reprint the text. At that time, the ideas contained in the book were too revolutionary for the USSR and its discovery carried the threat of imprisonment. Moreover, the book was intended for the future.

Only after the collapse of the USSR, when the storage and distribution of Helena Roerich's works ceased to be a punishable crime, was *Guidance for the Leader* finally published

---

[1] Incorporated Society for Psychical Research, "Madame Blavatsky, co-founder of the Theosophical Society, was unjustly condemned, new study concludes," press release, 8 May 1986.

in Russian. Helena Roerich's correspondence with President Franklin D. Roosevelt was also published and is now included in this English edition in the original.

When translating *Guidance for the Leader* into English, the translators endeavoured to preserve the author's unique style, at the same time making the text accessible to the English-speaking reader. In Russian, the book title is *Naputstviye Vozhdyu*. The very word *Naputstviye* in Russian has two meanings: parting words or wishes for one setting out on a journey, and guidance, advice, or recommendations (*nastavleniya*). In her correspondence, Helena Roerich often referred to the book as *Nastavleniya Vozhdyu*. Therefore, the word *Naputstviye* was translated in its second meaning of *Guidance*. It was also decided to refer to the Leader not only as *he*, as it is in the original language, but also as *she*. Helena Roerich especially emphasized the importance of women's leadership:

"The coming time should again give Woman a place at the helm of life, a place next to man, her eternal colleague, for all the grandeur of the Cosmos is based on these two Principles. The foundation of Existence represents the greatness of the two Principles. How is it possible to belittle one of them? All experienced as well as future disasters and cosmic cataclysms have the same cause — the humiliation of Woman.

"All terrible diseases, all the terrifying degeneration of many Eastern peoples, are based on the slavish dependence of women. A slave woman, deprived of the opportunity to enjoy the greatest human advantage — participation in creative thought and work, because in many countries she is deprived of the opportunity of equal education with a man and of revealing her abilities in building social and state life, of which she is a full member by virtue of the Cosmic Right. A slave woman can only give slaves to the world. The saying 'a great mother has a great son' has a profound scientific basis. For the son often borrows more from the mother, and daughters are the heirs of the father's powers. Cosmic Justice is great! By humiliating Woman, man has humiliated himself! … Would all the horrors and crimes that are committed now be possible if both Principles were balanced? Yes, the salvation of humanity and planet is now in the hands of Woman. …

"A woman who knows her high purpose, a woman who strives for beauty, for knowledge, will raise high the standard of living of any country, and there will be no place for all the heinous crimes resulting in the degeneration and destruction of entire nations."[1]

Of course, Helena Roerich's major work is the *Agni Yoga* series, or the *Teaching of Living Ethics*, written in collaboration with Mahatma Morya, and it is from here that she took many of the sections in *Guidance for the Leader*. However, this title also includes sections that cannot be found in the Teaching.

Agni Yoga represents a synthesis of all existing kinds of yoga. And this supreme form of yoga is essential today, when new fiery energies are incrementally reaching Earth from the Cosmos. This is what the people of antiquity were warning us of when they predicted the coming of the Age of Fire. While *Agni Yoga*, echoing ancient sacred scriptures, only warned humanity that "Fire is at the threshold!"[2] it is now prevalent on our planet. Thus, studies from the *Voyager* spacecraft now show that "tsunami waves" take place in the Solar System[3] which simply cannot but affect the Earth.

---

[1] Roerich, *Pis'ma*, vol. 1, pp. 89–90.

[2] Roerich, *Agni Yoga s kommentariyami*, vol. 2, pp. 148, 152.

[3] "Voyager Experiences Three 'Tsunami Waves' in Interstellar Space," *Jet Propulsion Laboratory*, https://www.jpl.nasa.gov/video/details.php?id=1347; "Sun Sends More 'Tsunami Waves' to Voyager 1," *Jet Propulsion Laboratory*, https://voyager.jpl.nasa.gov/news/details.php?article_id=38; "NASA Voyager: 'Tsunami Wave' Still Flies Through Interstellar Space," *Jet Propulsion Laboratory*, https://www.jpl.nasa.gov/news/news.php?feature=4411.

The ancient sages were aware that the Solar System has its own "seasons," which change depending on its location in the Cosmos and that last for millions of years. This knowledge is reflected, for example, in the four Yugas of Hinduism, which successively replace each other: Satya Yuga, Treta Yuga, Dvapara Yuga, and Kali Yuga, or Spring, Summer, Autumn, and Winter, respectively.

Modern astronomers have already determined that our Sun is moving in the direction of the constellation of Hercules.[1] Behind this constellation is the Central Spiritual Sun, which represents the invisible source of the most powerful Fire. In 1942, the Solar System saw the onset of the season of Cosmic Spring. And since 1999, it has entered a zone of increased influence of the currents of the Central Spiritual Sun and other invisible stars and planets.

It is these energies that cause climate change and global warming, when almost every subsequent year temperature records are broken. After all, how else can one explain the fact that warming is also happening on Mars, Jupiter, and Pluto?[2]

Moreover, the increased impact of the Cosmic Fire on our planet causes a "response" from its underground fire, or magma, which strives to merge with an energy similar to itself. The underground fire begins more actively to break through to the surface, both on land and at the bottom of the oceans.

---

[1] Nigel Henbest and Heather Couper, *The Guide to the Galaxy* (Cambridge: Cambridge University Press, 1994), p. 93.

[2] Ruth Marlaire, "A Gloomy Mars Warms Up," *NASA*, https://www.nasa.gov/centers/ames/research/2007/marswarming.html; Irene Klotz, "Radar Images Reveal Mars is Coming Out of an Ice Age," *Reuters*, https://www.reuters.com/article/us-space-mars-climate-idUSKCN0YH29N; Philip Marcus, "Velocities and Temperatures of Jupiter's Great Red Spot and the New Red Oval and Their Implications for Global Climate Change," *Bulletin of the American Astronomical Society*, vol. 38, p. 554; Robert Britt, "Global Warming on Pluto Puzzles Scientists," *Space*, https://www.space.com/3159-global-warming-pluto-puzzles-scientists.html.

However, in this natural process of energy exchange between the Earth and the Cosmos, humanity has introduced many violations with its low-frequency vibrations and destructive behaviour. This results in natural disasters the number of which has increased manyfold.

So, in order for humanity not to add fuel to the fire, but to save itself and the planet by establishing balance, Helena Roerich has left a tool for us in the form of *Agni Yoga* — a Teaching that allows everyone to master the most powerful elemental force, manifesting itself both in us and throughout the Cosmos. Indeed, the more people are able to assimilate the Fire, the more beautiful will be the future of their countries and the entire Earth.

Thus, from time immemorial to this day, Shambhala has never left anyone without its help and wise guidance — if only humanity could accept it.

∼

The preceding page shows the enhanced portrait of Mahatma Morya, which Helena Roerich received in Santa Fe, USA, on 11 October 1921 in a miraculous way. At the top of the original were the following words written in the Senzar language ꓕꓳꓮ̃ꓠ ꓶꓳꓥꓕꓭꓬ which mean "The Light of the Path" or "A Light-Guide."

Copies of this portrait were given only to the most trusted colleagues in America and other countries. It was Master Morya who guided President Franklin D. Roosevelt through Helena Roerich. It is also this portrait of the Great Lord of Shambhala that she sent to Roosevelt on 4 February 1935.

LETTERS
TO
FRANKLIN D. ROOSEVELT

NOTE

The letters below were written by Helena Roerich in English, which was not her native tongue. With the exception of punctuation, a few typos, and text in square brackets added for the sake of clarity, no other edits have been made to the original text.

October 10th, 1934

Mr. President,
At the austere hour when the entire world stands at the threshold of reconstruction and the fate of many countries is being weighed on the Cosmic Scales, I am writing to You from the Himalayan Heights, to offer You the Highest Help. The Help of that Source, which since time immemorial stands on constant Vigil, observing and directing the march of world events into saving channels.

History of all times and all peoples bears witness to this Help, which concealed from public notoriety, is usually extended at the turning point in the history of countries. The acceptance or rejection of this Help were inevitably accompanied by a corresponding flourishing or decadence of the country. This Help is made manifest in most unexpected and manifold aspects, through forewarnings and counsels. I shall not hold Your attention too long by enumerating the vast number of examples from the remote past, but I shall recall briefly a few nearest to our time. Thus the first Habsburg received a warning from a knight-singer; and the Norwegian King Knut met a stranger in pilgrim's garb, who summoned him to caution with his neighbours. And the King of Sweden Charles XII received a powerful warning from a priest not to begin the fatal attack against Russia, which put an end to the development of his country.

Since the publishing of the Diary of the Countess d'Adhémar, the lady-in-waiting to the ill-fated Marie Antoinette, the fact of frequent warnings by letters, personal visits conveying the warning about the danger threatening the country, the Royal House and their friends, has become broadly known. These forewarnings came invariably from the one Source — the Count [de] Saint-Germain, Member of the Himalayan Community. But all his saving warnings and advices were regarded as offences and fraud. Well known are to all the tragic consequences of this rejection.

Let us recall Napoleon, who during the first years of his glory liked to mention his Guiding Star, but who, nevertheless, did not accept the entire Advice, and driven by pride, went against the essential condition — his abstaining from attacking Russia. But he neglected the benevolent warning and the defeat of his army as well as his own tragic end are also well known. Amidst the more contemporary events, we can cite the warning given to Queen Victoria around 1850. The warnings and the wise Advice were rejected, and the consequences are taking their course.

To the Government of Russia were likewise timely given austere warnings and we are bearing witness to the grave results of rejection.

But let us now cite examples closer to You and examples of accepted Counsels. Thus we know that George Washington had counsel from a mysterious Professor and hence all his success. Likewise at the Declaration of Independence of America, during this Historical Assembly, the fact was registered as to how at the crucial moment of hesitation and indecisiveness, from amidst the audience rose a tall stranger who finished his flaming speech with the call: "America shall be free!" The enthusiasm of the Assembly was kindled and the Independence of America signed. When those present wished to greet him who helped them accept this great decision, the stranger could no longer be found; he had disappeared. Thus in the course of history, one witnesses how many variedly was manifested the Help of Warning and Counsel of the highest significance. And these Advices, coming from the Great Source, were always easy to carry out and had never demeaned that country to which they were extended.

In connection with the above-said, we should not forget the prophetic words of Abraham Lincoln about the threatening events which America will confront. These events have come, and the austere forerunners of the decisive hour are crowding at the threshold! And the same Source affirms: "America has reached the boundary of the turning point in her History. Precisely, America can reach her great significance and peaceful bounty. The Counsel is ready for America and it is useful for her to accept it, for else, many are the examples of grave consequences of rejection."

You, Mr. President, have realized that with the outlived measures, which have reduced the world to its present state of destruction, [it] is impossible to build the welfare and the future of the Country. You are indefatigably and courageously seeking ways of new constructiveness. You have understood that the Bird of Spirit of humanity cannot fly on one wing and hence you have given the due place to Woman. You can be not only the Ruler but the true great leader. Hence from the same One Source the Mighty Hand is outstretching to You Help and the Fiery Messages can once again reach the White House.

The map of the World is already outlined and it is offered to You to occupy the worthiest place in the forming New Epoch. And upon You depends to accept or to reject it. The destiny of the Country is in Your hands.

Who I am will tell You the carrier of this message. But I pray You to believe in the fiery striving of the heart, which aspires to help the Country and You, Mr. President, a heart which has joyously accepted the role of a Messenger of Good.

May your decision be for the best! For the acceptance of the Great Messages!

Helena de Roerich

November 15th, 1934

Mr. President,

Your message was transmitted to me. I am happy that Your great heart has so beautifully accepted the Message and Your light-bearing mind was free from prejudice, this horrible contagion which extinguishes in us the divine and creative fire of faith. Precisely Your faith in the New Constructiveness and Your open mind will help me to unfold before You gradually the entire Plan of the New Construction, in which You and Your Country are destined to play such a great part.

My heart rejoices to transmit to You the following Great Words: "Despite opposition, the Country knew not a more Beloved President. His fame will grow. It is thus Ordained."

Now I shall quote verbatim Indications received, referring to the most essential questions.

1. "Intentions are being nurtured to involve the country into war. The attempt will come from two sides. One attempt will come through a provocation from the land in the East, the other attempt through the instigation from the land beyond the ocean, on the ground of protection of China. Should even the opinion of the nation be in favour of war, one must not yield, for the Country faces reconstruction, which will place it on a height. These attempts must be vigilantly watched, for the pressure must be overcome. The Country must not disarm, on the contrary, let its might be felt. And though the nation may be against the armament, one must not give in, for no one will dare attack a mighty Ruler."

2. "The power beyond the ocean is an illusory power. This departing power does not nurture feelings other than hatred and jealousy towards Your Country."

3. "Many are the evil omens above the country of the East. The manifestation of Cosmic perturbations will shake its power. But vigilantly must the attempts be watched, for they

will result in war challenges. Thus let the President beware of conflicts. It is necessary that those who surround the President should not spread rumours about his unfriendliness to the land in the East, for they often give out their own opinion for the President's words. Thus this essential question is of primary importance."

4. "The Middle West of the U.S.A. is threatened with bad crops, hence it is useful to make provisions of grain and sow North and East; wheat may especially suffer."

5. "We send Musk to be taken when fatigued." — My entrusted one will transmit to You all indications about the properties of this wondrous remedy, which lends strength and balance to the nervous system as well as being a preventive against many ailments. In case You appreciate its effects, I shall be glad to send You more.

I shall end this message with the indication that in back of all the misfortunes of the Country, in back of all enemies of the Country stand those, whose name my entrusted one will reveal to You. But their downfall is decided, the coming decade will witness this great decline.

I know that Your great and valiant heart will manifest all possibilities for the preordained to be accomplished in all its might and beauty, therefore joy is abiding in my soul.

Austere is the time, but beautiful, for it is the time of the greatest Reconstruction in history and so many possibilities unfold before those, who proceed under the Protection of the Hand Holding the Helm of the World.

I am sending You, Mr. President, all the striving of my heart, all my best thoughts to help You in this predestined, great Achievement.

Helena Roerich

December 27th, 1934

With great joy in my heart I hasten to send the Reply.

"We see the possibility of establishing balance in the Neighbouring Countries and the people will remember the Initiator of this Unity of nations. We see a Confederacy of the Southern Countries of Am[erica], headed by the U.S.A. Work may begin in this direction. One need not hesitate because of the existing Pan Am[erican] Un[ion], for in its present state it represents a skeleton without a soul. We see a Union with Pr[esident] R[oosevelt] at its Head, consisting directly of the Heads of each Country. Its heart will be Pr[esident] R[oosevelt]. But in all this construction, the Pr[esident] will have to affirm the magnet of his heart, for its currents are mighty and the Pr[esident] must make use of them. *Nobody can replace him.* And We see how the Pr[esident] can pacify the conflicts between the Countries, if he will himself summon the Representatives of the Countries for arbitration.

"Let the Old House cease the policy poisoned by the Country beyond the Sea, for their venom penetrated into the soil of the Neighbouring Countries. All Cosmic conditions are propitious for secret negotiations of the Pr[esident], which must not be divulged by the Press nor by those who surround him. Hence must the Pr[esident] act through those who are devoted and sincerely attracted to him. Thus We see the construction of a Union, which will in the future annex S[outh] A[merica] to the U.S.A. and the Founder of this Great State will be Pr[esident] R[oosevelt]. This Great Union is designated and will be fulfilled.

"The Pr[esident] cannot discuss his plans in their completeness with anybody, but all channels must be led to this.

"One must likewise remember that the Elder in the Old House is by far more attracted to the interests of the Country beyond the Sea than to his own Motherland.

"Thus will the Pr[esident] be the Great Unifier of this mighty Country, which is destined to play a great role upon the Cosmic Scales. This vital question will be solved and Help will be Given to the Pr[esident]."

I must add that "the Country of the East traverses a difficult period of inner disintegration, which is skillfully concealed."

Likewise that "for the inner welfare of the Country a Control ought to be established which would supervise that the prices of products should not rise."

I shall be able to send you a special messenger with a Message.

To a heart aflame with true love for its Motherland, to a consciousness not poisoned by any prejudices nor afraid of vast horizons, the Answer is always ready.

The threatening signs of World-disintegration will be covered by the Construction of Light and upon the mighty foundation of the courage of Your fiery Heart and the great Trust in the Guiding Hand which rules the Destinies of the World, shall be built the Greatest of Epochs. Thus will the Predestined be fulfilled!

It is a joy for me to write to You this, it is a joy to trust Your Heart.

February 4th, 1935

Mr. President,

This message will be transmitted to You through my faithful Messenger. You can trust her just as much as my first Messenger. "Discrimination, vigilance, and silence" — are the foundations in the Great Service for the Welfare of humanity and they are fierily inrooted in our hearts.

In full trust and awareness of Your great Heart, I am transmitting to You, Mr. President, the following great Words:

"Thus it is predestined to President Roosevelt to build up America also during the next term, for the President will lay the foundation of the mighty and One America, hence can the President prepare for this date. Thus must the channels in this direction be created. The joy of the Nation will be the pledge for success. Now one may begin to prepare for the affirmation of the positions East, West, North, and South.

"The approaching decade will manifest many new foundations. Amidst the greed of many a nation will also be affirmed new designs.

"President Roosevelt manifests the essence of Uranus and his path is with the New Construction. The manifestations of many countries must now be looked upon from many angles. A hostile attitude will be shown to the Country on the part of Germany. France does not fully understand the spirit of the Country. The South too is following its own policy. The North can better understand the scope of the new construction. But the attention of the President must turn to the East. Speaking of the East, We have in mind also Russia. And in this direction the President should keep thus far a reserved attitude, since changes will take place.

"Thus must the Constructiveness be understood as an alliance of the countries in the Far East and in this union of the peoples of the East, the President is destined to bear a great part. While greedy nations will rely on the might of cannons, a Great State will be created in the East. This beginning will bring that equilibrium, which is so urgently needed for the construction of the great Future.

"America was since long ago linked with Asia. The ancient bonds were strengthened under propitious configuration of the Luminaries. That which is indicated by the Cosmic Laws ought to be created. One should not delay and impede the course of the Luminaries. Thus one must accept that the peoples occupying the larger part of Asia are destined to respond to the friendship of America. The President may accept the advice of happiness. Let the President's forces be applied towards the strengthening of the situation. By a firm hand the President may direct, at the appointed date, his peoples towards the Union which will give equilibrium to the World. One can apply small measures, but great measures should be realized. We are sending the Message that it might strain the will of the President and correlate it with the rays of the Luminaries. The peoples of America must enter a New Epoch. So-called Russia is the equibalance of America and only with such a construction will the World Peace become a solved problem. But the denial of highest principles cannot be a bulwark.

"Thus has come the time of reconstruction of the East, and let the friends of the East be in America. The alliance of the nations of Asia is decided; the union of the tribes and peoples will take place gradually; there will be a kind of Federation of countries. Mongolia, China, and the Kalmuks will constitute the counterbalance of Japan, and in this alliance of peoples, Your Good Will is needed, Mr. President. You can express Your Will in all its multiformity and the thoughts can be affirmed in this direction. Hence let the cultural construction begin in the heart of Asia. Nothing impedes America to adhere to Our direction. Let the cultural Corporation grow and the peaceful cooperation attract the nations. Many are the tribes which already aspire to adhere to Our action. Can America not adhere to the healthy structure? All Your signs, Mr. President, will become alive when the entire predestined fire will become aglow. Thus ought to be fulfilled the Ordainment of the Luminaries."

My heart is aflame with joy and faith in the great Construction with Your participation, Mr. President. Concerning some details of the great Plan, You can speak with my entrusted Messenger, as instructions will be transmitted to her. I beg of You, Mr. President, to trust my Messenger, for her loyalty is based on knowledge and tested not in times of happiness, but in the most difficult minutes and in the course of many years.

The Reconstruction of the World proceeds at a gigantic pace. The great Armageddon, which was foretold by all ancient Scriptures, is raging in its full power, and the forces of darkness, fighting for their very existence, apply all efforts to destroy every beginning of Light. Hence it is so necessary to watch vigilantly that the destroyers should not penetrate into the camp of Light. But Light conquers darkness, and the great Constructiveness *is approaching*.

I am sending You an ancient symbolic Image of the Lord of Shambhala and I beg You, Mr. President, to accept this dear and sacred to me Image and to remember that the Ray of the Great Lord will accompany You in all Your actions for the Good of Your Country and the establishing of the equilibrium of the World. Likewise is the wood-carved Figure of the Protector of Tibet, Bodhisattva Chenrezig, the symbol of the synthesis of the Cosmic Reason, which incarnates in the various races of humanity.

My Messenger will return to the Himalayas, hence Mr. President, Your questions and words can be transmitted to me in full safety.

The Great Trust is with You, Mr. President, and my heart rejoices to affirm this. The Chalice offered to You will bring You the Blessing of Nations.

I am sending You all the fire of my heart for the acceptance of the Highest Measure, the acceptance of the Chalice of the World.

In full trust,

Helena de Roerich

February 4th, 1935

Your question, Mr. President, reached our heights on the eve of the departure of my Messenger, and I am happy to add to the Message the Reply given to me:

"Europe shows signs of disintegration. The greed of Nations cannot be restrained by anything. But every usurpation will act as a rebounding blow, for, that which does not belong by right cannot be retained. Hence futile will be the attempts to bring to reason those whose actions are prompted by greed. For, often will these usurpations be launched as provocative challenges. Therefore it is best that the noble gesture of President Roosevelt should not be manifested publicly. These challenges of greed ought to be avoided. Let the dynamite explode there where it was planted.

"Our Ray is above President Roosevelt. A new Dawn rises above America.

"Thus will President Roosevelt be vested with Power."

Helena de Roerich

May 14th, 1935

The news about the great historical event — the Day of the Triumph of Spirit — has reached our Summits. The future nations will not forget that the Americas were the first to raise the Banner of Unity and Protection of Spiritual Treasures — this true heritage of humanity. Thus under this radiant symbolical Banner a new rapprochement of the nations of America took place — from the depth of my heart, I welcome your noble and wise gesture.

Now I hasten to transmit to you the following Great Words:

1) "The time has come and action should now be manifested. The fruit that is not plucked when ripe decays. The Great Pledge is given for the upbuilding of the New Country. The glory of America lies in the indicated direction. Trade, the safeguarding of the prestige, the opening of the new expansions will come only with the affirmation of the great construction in the heart of Asia. Not small nations, but a New Country will manifest its pledge of close friendship to him, who will stretch out his hand in full cooperation."

2) "The country of the East will experience five shocks. Soon new events will show that the foundations of the future should be laid. Therefore one should concentrate attention on the upbuilding of the New Country. The coming year (1936) is marked as the year of extraordinary opportunities and events. Let America take full advantage of the possibilities directed to her."

3) "The countries of the West will be engaged in great strife and

[The rest of the letter is missing]

December 1935

[Translated from the Russian due to
absence of the English copy]

Perhaps, this message will surprise You somewhat, but as always I write in total trust knowing that You will understand that what is said comes only from concern and the desire to do everything possible to protect You.

I ask that You no longer receive my first messengers, for nothing more will be transmitted through them. Those Who directed me to convey this to You have very special reasons for this. The one who hands You this letter is a friend of my family, but the contents of this letter remain unknown to her.

Often the things that are obvious hide the reality, but Those Whose gaze is directed towards causes, Who know the outlines of forthcoming Doom, again confirm everything that was said in my messages of February 4th and May 14th, and they point out the need at the very least to give moral support to those who now sowing the seeds of amicability towards Your country. Of course, the overseas State, together with the country of the East, observe vigilantly and attempt to sever threads of amicability towards Your country at every opportunity.

What is destined will be fulfilled, but Your country should not miss the best opportunities. Every grain of amicability will yield a rich harvest. And this amicability may be expressed in many ways. The difficulty of this construction is that he who is entrusted with the task of planting these seeds is not met with support from the country to which he so earnestly desires to bring the best. I am also instructed to warn You once again not to fix relations with the New Country too tightly.

H.R.

December 12th, 1935

In full confidence and with open heart, but this time in deep sorrow, I am writing to you. Already for several months I am seeking to find a possibility to warn you that the two persons, who had conveyed my messages, proved to be traitors in the fourteenth year of collaboration and I had to deprive them of my trust.

Having succumbed to covetousness and ambition they have broken the sacred trust and had transmitted to you in April their personal advice regarding certain financial matters (silver), pretending that it came from the Original Source through me. This Source warned me about the committed treason, and I was ordered to question them, and they both confessed to me in writing that they conveyed to you their own message, giving you the impression that it came from the Original Source through me. These letters are with me.

I was shocked and indignant at such treason and immediately cabled prohibiting to convey any message without my full knowledge and previous sanction. These two persons knew very well that all questions had to be referred to me, the more so as one of the two was to return here in the summer and to bring along any possible questions. When these persons saw my indignation at their action and realized the grave consequence of the latter they, moved by fear and revenge, turned to the path of open treason and decided not only to break all relations with us, but started an odious campaign to discredit our name in order to destroy us as witnesses of their deceitful action.

In their present hatred they stop at nothing. Mr. H[orch] took advantage of the absence on the expedition of the Founder of the Institutions and removed the Founder's name. Further Mr. H[orch], who had our full power of attorney since 1923 and who always attended to our personal accounts and taxes, suddenly after nine years, misrepresents to the Tax Dpt expedition funds for the years 1926 and 1927 (when we were in Tibet) as our personal income, misleading us all these years that tax matters were in order. As a result of his actions a lien without previous notification has now been placed on our property — our paintings — in America. These are but two instances of what they did to discredit our name. Such is the revenge of people, whose treason has been disclosed.

I am writing all this to forewarn you that Messages cannot be transmitted through these persons. The symbol of Judas and Devadatta is eternal; yet, no matter how difficult the times are for us at present, we know that truth and justice will prevail. Not easy is the path of those, who bring new ideas and lay the steps for the new consciousness of humanity. But ideas move the world and thus evolution takes place.

I am especially grieved that I could not warn you before and was unable to communicate with you, whereas my heart was longing to convey the Great Words at the threshold of the coming significant Year. No human reasoning can solve the present problems of the world. Only Those, Who stand on vigil, know whither the Wheel of Necessity rolls.

May the Blessing of the Highest rest with you.

I know that your great heart will understand.

In full trust,

P. S. If you approve this new channel, Messages could be sent again.

December 27th, 1935

"In the forthcoming events which will determine the course of the history of America it is essential to have President Roosevelt entrusted with the rudder. The national dignity as upheld by President Roosevelt will gain the hearts of the people. The masses uplifted by the noble formulae of the flaming heart of the President represent a force. Thus will the unprivileged support President Roosevelt.

"Agriculture is a powerful factor in the moulding of the course which will lead America to her great ultimate goal. With the welfare of the farmers the challenge of the enemies will be reduced to naught.

"There are threads which for a short period of time can be loosened. The firm hand will with ease restrain and righteously direct the forces with the victory gained.

"The foreign relationships demand constant watchfulness. The forces of disruption remain active as before — England, Germany, and Japan. The map of the world will be subject to many a battle. Although aloof from war America must stand as a powerfully armed and equipped country. Russia will represent the restraining force against Japan.

"The silver policy as directed by England has already dealt the rebounding blow to England. The basis of barter will bring beneficent results. Silver in America will always represent a secure backing.

"Thus with loyal spokesmen shall the distorting forces be defeated. And above all factors there reign supreme the noble and great achievements of President Roosevelt. Thus shall victory be with the flaming Heart."

New York,
December 27th, 1935.

January 11th, 1936

"The enemy could not have chosen a more dangerous path, a more absurd path than the battle waged against the welfare of the farmer. No weapon could be mightier than this opposition. Verily the nation will remember the motto of the flaming Heart — 'We shall not retreat.' Thus will Tactica Adversa be a powerful weapon. Victory will be with President Roosevelt.

"The principle of land conservation is a high aim and it will appeal to the nation. Glory to President Roosevelt.

"The fiery words of the President addressed to the nation have reached the hearts. All messages of the flaming Heart will act as a magnet."

New York,
January 11th, 1936.

GUIDANCE
FOR THE
LEADER

1933

THE WELL-BEING of whole nations forms around a single personality. There are numerous examples of this throughout history, in the most diverse of fields. Many will attribute this indubitable phenomenon to the personality as such. But this is the stance of the short-sighted. The more far-sighted understand that these assemblers represent nothing other than the power of the Hierarchy.

Indeed, in all phenomena, the Hierarchy chooses a focus towards which the current may be directed. Moreover, the personality of this category, consciously or unconsciously, possesses a fire that makes communication easy. However, another quality is required on the part of the people itself — their awareness and trust of the power in question. This constitutes a part of the fiery machine.

You yourself see how nations rise once a Leader is firmly established. You yourself see that it can be no other way. Thus it is important to acknowledge the link to the Hierarchy. Do not be short-sighted.

1. The Leader stands on a ridge with no downward slope. The born Leader has the ability to find the dividing line between opposites. It is from these mysterious lines that the carpets of victory are woven. Every day, every hour, a yarn of mysteries is unwinding before the Leader. Before her lies either leniency or connivance. Of course, the first gives birth to the second, yet between them lies the Sword of Justice, for leniency is of the Light, while connivance is of the darkness. The Leader's Sword lies on the ridge between the two.

Narrow is the place where the Sword may lie. Similarly narrow is the boundary between courage and cruelty. Only the heart of the Leader knows where this boundary passes. Not for great Counsels the riddle of the boundaries of Justice; the same riddles permeate all of life — hence for the Leader there is nothing small or great. The Leader's attention is equally acute in all her decision-making.

The Leader does not seek advice, yet she can accept it. The Leader is foreign to tardiness, and delays no one. She has the advantage of being able to appear unexpectedly and she knows how much time each task will take. She is not upset by slander, able to turn every word to her advantage. She is incorruptible, for she does not store up for herself earthly riches. As a healer of human hearts, she knows the significance of sound and colour. She rejoices at Truth, and rejects illusion. Thus, the path of the Leader is the path of Truth.

2. A loss of morale is not characteristic of the Leader, yet the pressure of a poisoned atmosphere may affect even a strong mind. Therefore, even the strongest Leader should not be left without cosmic support.

What can the Leader achieve if he is torn away from this life-saving connection? More than anyone, the one who takes on the burden of leadership must hold fast to the Ladder of the Supreme World. More than anyone, it is the Leader who must strengthen himself in his heartfelt work with emanations of Grace. He must address the Hierarchy in frequent conversation and take note of all the signs he is given, which the ignorant would negate as mere superstition.

Many useful observations have been undermined by a misunderstanding of what superstition really is. Sometimes, simply having your eyes open is called superstition, and yet the Leader must be above all superstition and prejudice. Let us imagine how life would change if we eliminated all prejudice, bias, and calculated decision-making. More than anyone, it is the earthly judges, who are given to endure the most burdensome weight of karma.

3. The Leader is not to be envied, for he bears all the heaviness of life. One might recall how, when greeting a certain Victor, an old woman wept bitterly. When asked: "Why the tears" amidst the common joy, she said: "I feel so sorry for him."

4. One may ask, why I speak of the *Leader*, and not the *ruler*? There is an enormous difference between the two. The term *ruler* implies primarily the present — and the governing of something that already exists, while the *Leader* — quite literally — reveals the future. She is not in receipt of something already formed, she *guides*, and her every action propels the people forward. While the ruler knows everything about that which is formed and finished, the Leader has nothing pre-established and must lead the people towards the Mount of Perfection. While the ruler's burden is great, the responsibility of the Leader is even greater.

This notwithstanding, the Forces of the Highest consolidate their throne where there are signs of leadership. The Leader must discern between pretence and sincerity. The virtues of the heart have nothing in common with forced obsequiousness, and the Leader has the power to distinguish between these qualities.

Many have read how David enquired of the Supreme Forces. He turned to this Source to avoid making unnecessary mistakes. Such examples are numerous in the history of many different nations. They are known to us all. You do not have to immerse yourself in ancient times to find them, for such signs of Communication and Service to the Great can be seen just as well in contemporary events.

However, we also know that Great Communication requires a pure heart. Communication cannot be granted to anything impure; therefore, the Symbol of Leader must be the sign of a pure heart. Not only in her actions but in her thoughts, too, the Leader brings the good to the people. Knowing that she is charged with carrying the full cup, she does not roam and therein lose the path; she will not spill the entrusted chalice. Thus the concept of *Leader* is a sign of the Future.

5. Remember how much people need the concept of *Leader*. They want to have a guarantor before the Supreme; they know how impossible it is to find the path without a connection, yet they are aware that the Leader will come. Nothing can ever impede the Leader, provided that he remains undeterred by any everyday manifestation that would engender his retreat; pure aspiration in the Leader can never be prematurely curtailed.

6. Naturally every Leader will encounter a multitude of circumstances along the way that may make their karma more difficult. This is inevitable, and no ordinary, everyday decision has the power to dissolve such pressure. Why would the Leader take upon herself any unnecessary burden, when she is in Communication with Higher Powers? She does not increase the weight of her karma when she executes the Behest of the Higher Powers.

Yet to retain such a fortunate position she must gather and direct her whole mind towards the World of the Most High. She must become free of any obstructive habit and reform her will, placing it in indissoluble contact with her Guide. She must become accustomed to this Communication, so that it becomes the integral foundation of her life. In addition, the Leader should not conceive of revenge, for this is a most animal feeling. The Leader has no time for vengeance if she knows no infringement, for she is in constant motion. The Leader also knows that rest is nowhere permitted, for it is the killing of energy. Likewise, the Leader understands that doubt is not the search for truth. Anyone who peers into the distance aspires towards the Truth; yet whoever doubts turns back, and therein meets with peril.

7. Impermeable armour can be made of metal or silk, but the best armour is of fire. Can the Leader really traverse the destined path without fiery armour? How else is he to avert the arrows of malice and swords of hatred? Many Leaders, even with their earthly consciousness, have sensed that they were protected by a fiery armour.

One could write whole books about the magnetism of the destined Leader. Note that the people are convinced not by appearance, voice, or even riches, but by something else. I have spoken before about the Fire of the heart on more than one occasion. This is the armour-magnet that both attracts and protects. As the phrase goes: "I shall accept all arrows into my shield." But first you have to forge the shield. This is a shield that can come only from Above, and yet there are so many thoughts and conversations that must be had in order to create the Communication and forge this fiery armour! You must not waste a single day, a single hour if you wish the Communication to be living and everywhere present.

They are mistaken, those who think that science distances one from the Supreme World; science may change the names of earthly things, but the triune essence is unalterably its foundation. Moreover, the Leader is able to envision where essence resides. He may not utter a single word, but he will feel it in his heart. The word itself will help prevent the Leader from losing a universal understanding; this alone easily affords a marvellous armour.

8. The Leader is aware that she confronts the forces of darkness. The Leader recognizes that the fight against them is merciless. The Leader knows how cunning are the tricks of the darkness, yet she has two weapons against it. The first is her vigilance and moderation in life; the second is her Communication with the Forces of Light in all their Invincibility. It is no small joke to stand before all the horrors of darkness, and not turn away. But the Leader feels the Guiding Hand, and in battle she senses this Hand — or light touch of Grace — descending upon her brow. The Leader will not miss these signs of Grace. The Leader must help the people and purify meaning in the distorted expression of ideas. To a large degree, most discord in life stems from confused concepts. Hence, experts in language should be brought together to purify the meaning of words.

9. The Leader should encourage, should be capable of discerning true talent, and assign tasks accordingly. Giving worthy praise is the garden of gratitude, but it has already been said that gratitude is a bridge that leads towards the Supreme Light.

10. The Leader determines the cycle and measure of things with the heart. This knowledge is not the arbitrary kind. Established Communication with the Hierarchy provides the Leader with immutable knowledge concerning the future. Foresight is a Leader quality and yet where can this prescience originate if the Higher Gates remain closed? How can one create an understanding of cycles if the Leader fails to notice the flowing of the stream? Can the human mind really grasp all that the Leader sees? Is human pride really so great that it will place itself above all else? The ignorant may be unable to understand where cycles and measure originate, but the enlightened consciousness is familiar with the Hierarchy of Light.

11. The connection of closeness, like the law of attraction, is clear to both priest and scientist. So how does the choosing take place? In the same way that vibration separates and unites grains of sand into certain patterns — you can see how some rush to unite — these images of rhythm do not illustrate separation at all. Instead they affirm the consonance of potential combinations.

"O Fiery Heart, hasten to align yourself with the cosmic rhythm and strengthen in your being the beauty of the pattern of Existence."

12. Can one really call tyrant anyone who cares about amity? Can one really use this term to describe someone who encourages cooperation? Can such a label be pinned on someone who aspires to knowledge? Can we apply it to someone who promotes creativity? Or to someone who deepens their striving for self-improvement?

Of course, the ignorant who are married to the darkness fear all affirmations of Light, yet these small vipers will burn in the Fire of the Leader's heart. Many names will be written on sheets of paper, but even three hundred and sixty sheets would only remind us of the Leader who is to come. A special education of the heart is needed to recognize the features of the Leader who is to come. Only Communication with the Hierarchy can consolidate unwavering advancement towards the Light. Who will find the strength to look at the radiance of the Light if their eyes have never known the brilliance of the Ladder of Ascent?

13. Homeland establishes a person's magnetic attraction to a particular quality of spirit. You can impoverish this concept with hypocrisy, but Higher Communication enables an enrichment of the earthy homeland through expansion of consciousness. Whereas the earthly motherland attracts the individual, it is but a starting-point for Infinity. Does it denigrate the earthly homeland to compare it with Infinity? On the contrary, every exaltation is worthy of the Leader's heart.

14. The desire to help adorns the Leader. How many opportunities are born of this noble desire! Many desires degenerate into passions, yet the desire to help is at the root of selflessness.

15. Peoples who find joy in labour have the right to expect of the Leader a fair assessment of their work. The Leader should have a decent understanding of labour as a core value. The Leader should be able to discern the expression of true merit — be it mental, creative, or muscular. Joy must result from labour. Providing a variety of educational spectacles and discussions is also a means of clear and calming leadership.

You can understand that peoples who find joy in labour know no retired colleagues. Social support is required only in cases of disease or infirmity. There can be no question of resignation when one's strength is not exhausted, for labour is joy. It is not possible to deprive people of work, instead, one should select labour that is appropriate to their nature.

This will require a Council of educated scientists who are able to judge wisely, without superstition or prejudice. The Leader should select the members of the Council, and it is his responsibility to keep it closed to the ignorant and other servants of the darkness. It is inconceivable that labour and cooperation should end up in the hands of the ignorant and be associated with self-interest. Labour is a measure of quality of consciousness. Work should lead one's conscious mind towards self-perfection, for then labour, as the Banner of Ascent, will deliver joy and health. Thus, first and foremost, the Leader is Patron of labour and he himself is able to rejoice in his work.

16. You will always find those who chant: "Down with the Leaders, down with the Teachers, down with the Rulers!" Know that they are parasites that feed on disturbance and decay. Falsehood and infringement are the nature of parasites; they secretly collect riches and are not averse to reaping luxury. So you need to be capable of distinguishing those who are by nature builders from those who are destroyers. Hence it is just to associate with those who know the joy of labour, those who are acquainted with Leaders and revere Teachers, for their very nature aspires towards cooperation.

17. Miracles are living. Life is worth living through the perception of miracles. Numerous existing combinations are broken on account of stupid negation and shameful blindness of consciousness.

18. Absolute equality of gender and ethnic groups lies at the foundations of state. The Leader must take full responsibility for compliance with these principles. No remnants of the past should interfere with what is confirmed by Nature herself.

19. Swiftness in legal proceedings will lift the spirits of the population. The Leader must carry responsibility for ensuring that Justice is administered without delay. Judges must be tested not only in their knowledge of formulas, but in terms of their ability to comprehend the human heart. Various experts may be consulted, yet the judges themselves must possess a sufficiently enlightened consciousness. The Leader herself must examine the consciousness of the judges. Justice is a manifestation of the nobility of the state.

20. No one should know the Leader's daily schedule in its every detail, for the population may wait for him every hour in the expectation of help and encouragement. At dawn and at midnight, none will refuse an audience with the Leader. Also, the means of travel should be chosen by the Leader without prior planning, and both attendants and attire should be approved by the Leader himself.

21. The Leader is not only concerned with the physical health of the people, she protects their spiritual strength, too. She understands the need for freedom of spiritual belief. She gathers together Councils of wise individuals to make sure that spiritual freedoms are not violated, for spiritual freedoms are the wings of the people.

22. Banknotes should be of two kinds: one for foreign circulation and the other, domestic. Such internal notes or cooperative certificates contribute much to the development of domestic industry. They also help in the exchange of goods and handicrafts. The quantity of such notes need not be limited, being conditional upon the production rates of each individual country.

Thus, every citizen of the state may have three sources of income: First, a small amount of foreign currency, which may be added to as a result of special tasks approved by the state; second, internal certificates secured through labour; third, the exchange of various goods and products.

23. Education of the people should start with the primary upbringing of children, from the earliest possible age; the sooner the better. Trust that mental exhaustion results only from sluggishness. Every mother, when approaching her baby's cradle, should utter the first formula of education: "You can achieve anything." There is no need for prohibitions. Even harmful things should not be forbidden; it is better to divert the child's attention towards something more useful and attractive. The best upbringing is one that exalts the attractiveness of the good. At the same time, one should avoid distorting beautiful images, as it were, in the name of a child's lack of understanding. Do not degrade children! Hold firmly to the thought that true science is always attractive, concise, accurate, and beautiful. It is necessary for families to have at least a germ of understanding about education. After the age of seven much may already be lost.

Usually after the age of three the body is full of perceptions. At a child's very first step the hand of the guide should turn their attention to higher concepts and point out Distant Worlds. Young eyes should be trained to sense Infinity. And it is specifically the eyes that should become accustomed to acknowledging the Infinite.

Also, words should be used to express precise thought. Falsehood, rudeness, and mockery should be excluded. Betrayal, even in thought, is inadmissible. Working "like the grown-ups do" is encouraged. Only the consciousness of a child up to the age of three can easily grasp the concept of *cooperation*. How erroneous it is to think that you need to give every individual child their own things, for children easily grasp the notion that all things may be shared.

The awareness that "I can achieve anything" is not a boast, but simply a realization of the apparatus. Even the most miserable soul can find a thread leading to Infinity, for all labour, in its individual quality, can open the gates to Infinity.

24. Education in primary and secondary schools should be the same for both genders. One must not impose a speciality on children when they have not yet discovered their own abilities. Secondary school is sufficient to divide the educational programme according to an individual's talents. The secondary school system makes it possible to combine the education of those who cannot discover their potential this early. It is very important that the curriculum be the same for both genders. This condition alone will erase the extremely harmful attitudes that exist towards gender.

25. School curricula should be examined with a view to intensifying the best direction for sound learning. The idealism of superstition is enough to drive people to the verge of horror. This correction of school thinking should be carried out immediately; otherwise, yet another generation of dimwits will disgrace the planet.

It is necessary to strengthen *natural science* after grasping the meaning of this phrase. Biology, astrophysics, and chemistry attract the attention of the youngest brain. Allow children the opportunity to think for themselves. Also, the primary school level programmes should be deepened. This advice should be implemented without delay.

26. All obsolete subjects must be removed from the curriculum. Ancient languages should be optional. Introduce instead the study of general linguistics. Of course, the curriculum will change according to the needs of the population. Visual learning, natural sciences, geography, applicative knowledge, and crafts should be especially developed. Spiritual conversations should be introduced in the spirit of various religions, depending on pupil composition. The difference between rural and urban secondary schools should be eliminated. Primary school education should be accessible to all, likewise, secondary school and university.

Pay particular attention to primary school education. In primary schools, pupils should study jointly up to the age of ten. Secondary school education should run from the age of ten to sixteen, although naturally, depending on pupil ability. There should be no joint studying in secondary school. There should be no exams; instead, all pupils should submit individual work carried out during the year. Let even the seven-year-old demonstrate what they can do. This method makes it easier to judge a child's abilities. Schools should be the most beautiful of buildings.

Spiritual discussion should take place in a special room, hung with the portraits of all founders of different religions.

In addition, schools must not kill individuality of spirit. Of course, all politics should be excluded. I consider summer camps to be highly beneficial. Military schools should be abolished, but military discipline can be introduced in schools. A Military Academy should be established — a University equivalent institution — for those who wish to devote themselves to military affairs. Those who join the Academy should be exempted from military service, and their term of study counted as service; the remainder should serve as usual.

Women should take part in the municipal economy.

27. The task of a true school is to direct the consciousness of its pupils towards the future. Nobody wants to accept the idea that the shifting of awareness towards the future is to create a guiding magnet. The point is that awareness must be fully directed towards the future. Many believe that it is sufficient that they think about the future sometimes, and then return to bathing in the past. One should give to the future not just a few isolated thoughts — the very essence of the conscious mind

should be attuned to the stream of the future. It is important not to force yourself into such a transformation; this can be achieved only by coming to love the future. There are not many that love the future. A country that knows joy in labour, may be carried naturally into the future while focusing on perfecting the quality of their labour. It is incumbent upon the Leader to lead the people towards the future.

28. Evolutionary world processes should be expounded in schools in a highly engaging manner. The motherland takes its shape from world processes and should therefore occupy an attributable place and significance. Every individual must know the true value of their fatherland, yet it should not be presented as a tree growing in the desert — it has its own cooperations with multitudes of other peoples. Likewise, belief in Supreme Justice will come from knowledge of reality. Let the processes of the world find living interpreters. The Leader himself must be vigilant to ensure that the great paths of nations are not distorted in favour of ignorance.

29. Any unification can take place only on the basis of cooperative principles. Admit the element of conquest, suppression, and humiliation, and these revolting shadows will sooner or later transform into destructive monsters. Therefore, no violence can be included in the construction of the stronghold. The power of joy may be found in collaboration, but such collaboration requires the art of thinking.

Who should distribute the forces of productive labour? Only one who is able to imagine effective collaboration. This person must be capable of visualizing such collective work, and yet, as you already know, imagination must be cultivated. The task of every school is to open up a well-grounded imagination.

30. Any movement tending towards a labour strike is unacceptable, as it signifies the destruction of production processes. Such acts of madness can occur only in states of the coarsest form. Humanity stands at a sufficient stage of reason to understand how to eliminate disputes by means of reasonable discussion. Any destructive condition must be urgently resolved. There can be no talk of collaboration in a condition of enmity. Reasonable forces must unite in order to avert the threat of catastrophe. If technological advances were coupled with spiritual understanding, a balance would be achieved much more easily.

31. In addition to cooperatives, there should be fraternities for cultural communication. Few will understand where the borderline between a business cooperative and a fraternity of culture should be drawn. But every school, every institution is capable of bringing together a circle of individuals that are capable of aspiring towards spiritual perfection. There is a need to favour unity in every way possible. Entire staff of mobile teachers should attend these Fraternities and contribute the joy of learning. The government should encourage the education of these group members. They may be different kinds of specialists, but when on leave, they should devote some of their time to attending these Fraternities. It is essential that the teachers have diverse specialties, for only then can they explain diverse interpretations of attractive discoveries and achievements in a variety of fields.

Children especially need to be encouraged in their aspirations to improve life. Prizes may be awarded to young inventors, although efforts in this area should not be limited to the technological sphere of life alone. Such improvements can be carried out everywhere, even in spiritual domains — this will bring the mind of the people out of slumber. Indeed, in its essence, each improvement is positive. Only through a continuous, engaging movement is it possible to achieve national prosperity.

32. How differently our building plans develop! We used to say: "Give everything away." Now We go even further and say: "Take everything, but do not think of it as your own."

Even an ordinary mind will understand that it is impossible to take earthly things with you. Yet they have been created with the participation of spirit and, therefore, should not be disregarded. How can one pass by the flowers of Nature? The creations of labour are the flowers of humanity. If their scent and colour are imperfect, have compassion.

33. It is good to understand how to possess things without a feeling of ownership. It is good to possess things — to take care of them, even imbue them with a benevolent aura, with the intention of passing them on to others. The hands of creativity dwell in a house without being attached to the property and, once improved, the house will bring additional joy. And the mark of a giving hand will remain continuously — herein lies the justification of things. This understanding will help solve the most difficult of questions. I say this for the world, since the world's greatest danger lies in its attachment to non-existent property. Communicating this to people will completely eliminate their fear of old age.

The concept of possession without ownership will open for all the path to unconditional inheritance. Whoever is able to improve something will possess it. Likewise, this applies to land, forests, and water sources. Various kinds of invention as well as all the achievements of technology are subject to the same concept. It is not difficult to imagine how national creativity will be activated, especially when one is aware that spirit alone offers the best solutions.

Questions will indeed stretch to the hearth of spirit — which way is best? And the swords of spirit will defeat guile. Truly, it is advantageous to do better. The law is simple, as with everything in spirit.

34. When difficulty with an inheritance arises, you could say: we can do without wills but may leave a directive to the state to transfer the right to use certain things to a designated person for a three-year probationary period. Thus, the inheritance will be transformed into an agreement among worthy persons. Special electors could be appointed to monitor work quality. It is useful to deepen awareness of constant testing, for the people are not yet capable of working in this way. All the substances of the world are mutually tested. The concept of *testing* should be understood as "improvement."

35. Aspiration towards true cooperation lies at the foundation of evolution. The cooperative system is the only salvation. Destruction of the path of ignorance is possible through the awakening of creativity alone. Even if its forms are monstrous. Even if they do try to make a sun out of a candle-lighter in the back yard, still a raging torrent will break through the wall of matter. New findings will intensify the spirit of gathering. Instead of stock-market speculation, let there be striving for discovery, supported by cooperatives.

36. Do not live on proceeds derived from money. Profit such as this is impure. Better, the movement of goods through the exchange of commodities; as a last resort, it is admissible to exchange money that is immediately convertible.

Criminal speculation must be prosecuted relentlessly, for the Earth is sick with speculation. Each epoch has its own disease — today the Earth is sick with speculation. It is wrong to think that humanity has always been susceptible to this disease. It is a sign of significant change, for it cannot pass gradually, and a paroxysm of evolution is needed to defeat this infection.

37. Monetary alms must be eliminated. Help should take the form of work or things. When people proceed along the path of spirit, there will be no unemployment. Our task is to show the benefit of perfection, not for the sake of the Invisible World, but for our own sakes.

38. The key misunderstanding will surround the idea of labour as rest. Many forms of entertainment will have to be abolished. The main thing is to understand that the purpose of works of science and art is educational and not for entertainment. Many forms of entertainment must be eradicated, for they are hotbeds of vulgarity. The vanguard of education must cleanse the dens full of fools sitting over a beer. Likewise abusive language must be met with a more severe punishment. Similarly, narrow specialism should be disapproved of.

39. Let us honour the Leader with our whole understanding. Let us support the Leader who maintains constant fervency through success and failure. The Leader bears the flame of the ever-burning heroic deed. The teaching of life can be interrupted neither by fatigue nor disappointment. The heart of the Leader lives by the heroic deeds of the people. She has no fear, and the words "I am afraid" have no place in her vocabulary. Her example ignites a very bright light and creates the people's consciousness.

The hands of the Leader never rest. The head of the Leader supports the heaviness of activity. The Leader's powers of reason seek out firm solutions. The power of her experience overcomes the weakness of others. At the border of loss, she creates new opportunities. On the line of retreat she builds strongholds. In the face of the enemy she unfurls her Banner. A day of fatigue, she calls a day of rest. She is as willing to accept misunderstanding as she is to accept rubbish on her threshold. She can hide the sacred in the folds of her work clothes. For the Leader a miracle is but the print of a horseshoe. For the Leader, determination is but her daily bread!

40. The Leader lays four stones at the foundation of his actions. The first is the veneration of the Hierarchy. The second is the awareness of Unity. The third is an understanding of Commensurability. The fourth is the application of the canon "by thy God."

41. The Leader is distinguished by the discipline of freedom. Not only is her spirit disciplined, but the quality of her external actions, too. To be excessively sad is not customary for the Leader. Nor is it her wont to count on people too broadly. She is not in the habit of expecting too much. It is often necessary to replace a complicated plan with a simpler one, but never the other way round. Only adversaries move from the simple to the complex.

42. Demonstrate discipline of spirit, for without it you will never be free. For the slave, spiritual discipline is a prison; yet for the one who is free, it is a healing garden of beauty.

Whoever understands the discipline of spirit will understand the direction of Fire and adopt the concept of *cooperation for the Common Good*. The road's end may be illumined by a thousand fires of Common Good.

43. A clear and concise command may be difficult, but it is stronger than a magic wand. An affirmation may be easier, but a command is like a sudden pillar of flames rising up from a volcano. In a command there is a concentrated feeling of personal responsibility; in a command there is the indication of inexhaustible strength. The determination of the Cosmos is manifested in the fury of the command, like a crushing wave. Wipe away your tears of goodness; we need the sparks of an indignant spirit!

Regrets create such a dam, but wings grow at the tip of a sword!

44. Make sure that commands are prepared in advance and can, therefore, enter the consciousness of those who will execute them. Without cooperation a command is like an arrow set flying against the wind. Even the unexpectedness of an order must be foreseen. Then the unexpectedness will be transformed into a weathered tension.

The Leader is able to foster cooperation not only in actions but in thinking. Only then can a colleague be trusted to work independently in the field. The attribution of an assignment obliges a person to undertake independent action. The flow will carry those who strive.

45. Encouraging spiritual individuals is something that can be learned. While they do not perform heroic deeds of spirit for the sake of encouragement, they still need it to maintain their spiritual direction. Every Ruler must know the power of reproach, but also understand the benefits of encouragement; the latter being the more difficult. Much Grace emanates when a Ruler knows what each individual requires for their "Lotus" to blossom. One may have many hermits, but their noble intensity will not yield the supreme measure of energy if surrounding forces are hostile. Therefore, the Leader must strengthen the heart in its aspiration to understand the very best.

46. Poor is the Leader who conceals a real danger, for only with complete knowledge of it can a danger be overcome.

Without fear and as far as possible alone — this is how the Leader should act. Expressions of personal responsibility are correct, not miracles or quotations, but assertions strengthened by personal example. An error made in daring is more easily rectified than stooped mumbling! Action is precious that does not depend on apparatuses or assistants! Anyone who discovers a precious formula must resist the temptation to shout it from the rooftops, as falling into the hands of those with less pure motivations, the harm created will outweigh any benefit.

The Leader stands like a sealed vessel, an unspoiled mountain, like a bow stretched taut with loaded arrow. And he acts as if the vessel contained a flaming drink, the mountain were inexhaustible, and the arrow were lethal. For who would dare assert that overcoming difficulty is not the swiftest form of achievement! Rivers of milk may turn sour, and honeyed shores may be uncomfortable to sit upon. And so, the Leader hastens into the armour of personal responsibility.

Luck is only found where there is absolute courage. Petty doubts give birth to slavish fearfulness.

47. When a physician foresees the flow of a disease, you take the proposed measures. When an astronomer foresees a solar eclipse, you stock up on the appropriate lighting. But when a social psychologist foresees the course of events, you scream, "Prophet!" and in terror hide in the most stinking of corners. Of course, you do this allegedly to preserve scientific methods, but in reality, hypocrisy and fear prevent you from pondering where there is truer knowledge — in the short-sighted judgement of the physician creeping along the peripheral covers or in the far-sightedness and accuracy of the social seer, in whom experience is combined with cogency?

Recall your social prophets who indicated the events of humanity centuries in advance. You do not refer to them as mystics or hypocrites. Like Us, you refer to them as far-sighted psychologists. On this definition We shall settle and are in agreement. As an aside, it is worth noting that the meaning of the widely condemned word *prophet* is "one who predicts." The true Leader always predicts the course of events, which suggests that the concept is no less real than medicine or astronomy.

48. Observe indications of seismic curves. They are not located along the equator, or along the meridian, but form their own curve. Sometimes intensified activity of quakes and shifts coincides with the tension of so-called sunspots, which results in increased tension in the Solar System. It does not take a prophet to understand that brain activity will function differently during these cycles.

Social aspirations also have their own distribution curve. One must be careful not to interrupt the sequence of events. Fissures created by shifts are the same, be they in the soil or in people's aspirations. A nation's Leader must stand at the crest of new horizons. The New World must display the sensitivity of our best seismographs.

Anyone who complicates the procession of peoples may be awarded the wreath of ignorance. For the Leader ignorance of the laws can be no excuse any more than it is acceptable for a driver to go against the flow of traffic. None should be guided by personal considerations, yet, by comparing individual values with the common good, one may choose the most expedient path. One must be careful not to waste a single opportunity.

This may sound like a simple boring truth, but no one applies it, and the plan of action is made in a darkened room, not from a watchtower. One should observe not how you want things to be, but how things are in reality.

49. The builder must know what weight the house pillars can bear. Incommensurability results in destruction, blasphemy, falsehood, betrayal, and all sorts of unseemly phenomena.

Can a building really stand where the properties of a giant are ascribed to a flea, where a poker is sought after more ardently than the Lord, where a whirlwind is compared to the flight of a mosquito?

The conditions of construction are total commensurability of thought and expression — this is the stronghold of the truth of beauty. Practising this in life is easy without reticence or exaggeration.

The Leader observes his colleagues closely to make sure that the way they express themselves corresponds with meaning. Only in this way can different beings cooperate.

The best judgement will be by beauty, for it is coarse to say: "I'll put a giant into a small casket" or "the eagle soars like a hen"!

How often the best devices are destroyed by incommensurability, which is easily avoided with a little attention.

50. What suffers most? Commensurability. When commensurability is ignored, determination is destroyed. The determination of the Leader must extend to the absolute limit. This is not the kind of determination that proceeds comfortably and conforms to habits. Nor is it the kind that is good for the body. The determination of the Leader is restricted only by the limitations of spirit. Therefore, it is impossible to block the aspiration of the Leader. Builders and assemblers proceed with this kind of determination.

51. Alongside *commensurability*, there should also be an understanding of *necessity*. The final test will be the test of necessity; in other words, everyone tested must say what they consider to be the most necessary. Their consciousness will be measured by the quality of their immediate answer.

They will ask: "With what should each action begin?" From the most necessary, for each moment has necessity, and this is known as the *rightness of action*.

Hence even a spirited horse can sense with the tip of its hoof which stone to first step on. In this same way is the order of mobility, commensurability, and necessity to be felt.

52. Degree of usefulness may change. After all, degrees of usefulness are as many in number as the leaves on a tree.

53. It is important to distinguish things that are imitable from things that are unique. One may put aside the things of everyday life, but the call of a new cycle should be taken up without delay. You could say that the moment of cosmic opportunity is irreplaceable. Certain foods can be digested only in a certain order. And a hunter does not go hunting on account of idleness.

54. A heroic deed is never an act of renunciation; it is assimilation of knowledge with movement, so when I say "one who has renounced," you should take this to mean "one who has assimilated." It is impossible to imagine the essence of renunciation, for prohibition nestles beside it, while assimilation points to conscious realization.

Once a Leader has grasped the grandeur of future construction, nothing can hinder the growth of her spirit.

Faithfulness is a quality inherent in a high-frequency spirit, and the process of assimilation makes the truly heroic deed a joyful achievement. Thus the heroic deed can evolve, for one light-bearing achievement entails another.

Aspire to the future, bypassing the soot of the present.

You need to know how to avoid causing destruction by summoning the upmost patience.

55. You must learn to avoid the standard benchmarks of life. The best people get ahead of the world that is weighed down by dark clouds. Whoever wishes to reach a New Land must not only cast away all prejudice but also enter by a new path.

The affirmation of life should be built on the observance of local conditions. Where there are one hundred different languages, one must understand one hundred different mentalities. Having one approach for all is like the banal standard design columns used in all government facilities. Unity in diversity yields the harvest.

56. It sometimes happens that the surest plan encounters difficulties. They will ask, "How do we find a solution without expending excessive amounts of energy?" A change may be made to the essence of the plan, or to its dimensions or location. Altering the very essence of a plan is tantamount to betrayal. Curtailment of the plan in its dimensions equates to short-sightedness. The Leader's decision should consist in changing location, so that new foundations can deepen the fundamental meaning even more. The basic principle "to fight to the death" should be rejected. It is more courageous to win without sacrificing one's strength. But to do this one must thoroughly understand the rightness of the aspiration, the total immovability of one's determination.

How fortunate it is if a new place can be found that deepens the potential of the previous location. The Leader does not limit the plan through the choice of place alone — it is the essence of the plan that is essential.

57. A word on the immutability and agility of the plan: these conditions are particularly difficult to combine, although their meeting point can be clearly delineated by a distinct understanding of the ray of solar consciousness. To realize a plan in life, one must be ready to be mobile at any hour.

This seeming variability consists in nothing more than the vibrations of life. The paths to the milestones of immutability breathe and surge like waves.

When approving a plan, the Leader's whole being is set to take the shortest path. Mobility can arise only from an awareness of the plan's immutability.

58. A word on the incommensurability of cycles. Small streams of events are given alongside ocean waves. Can a little brook really be taken for an ocean? But on Earth people always hasten to confuse the personal with the global. As the hand feels the thickness of a fabric, so the spirit must discern the depth of events.

The Leader should not be carried away by the seeming magnitude of an event, for between the main knots there may be many-coloured phantoms, and streams may temporarily change their channels. A nodal wave raises a boat for an instant, but before each subsequent wave it becomes still. The most sensitive boat will shudder ever more strongly, for the dust of the explosion fills the atmosphere. Hence the commensurability of cycles and events must not be forgotten.

Like deceleration, the good fortune of acceleration comes in waves. Having spotted an accelerating wave, you should throw into it as many seeds as possible.

59. During construction, the Leader observes that no self-interest should be found hiding beneath the guise of carrying out commandments. Dark self-interest entails the destruction of creative achievements. I say: this worm is much too characteristic of human baseness. All the more reason to know the cause of its origin.

The most significant cause will consist in privilege. This harmful ghost must be destroyed at all cost. First and foremost, cooperation provides for equality. Once you err and undermine equality, you immediately run up against destructive privilege. The manifestation of inequality creates swings. The great rise of one only generates a great rise in the other. The only way to eliminate the shaking of the pillars is to maintain equality.

The cynics will say: "Let them swing — there will be more energy in space." Such a remark is not entirely devoid of logic, yet the cause of construction requires such care that true economy of strength should be permitted. Equality is the most economical of principles as it eradicates privilege and self-interest.

60. Genuine selflessness is a true fire-flower, yet it must be manifest not only in a person's deeds, but in their very consciousness. Deeds, like wandering shadows, are reflections, and the whirlwind of reverberating conventionalities conceals the meaning behind our actions. Can an action really be judged without knowing its cause and effect? If so, then a saviour may be judged an offender, and a giver may appear a miser. It is not easy to acquire the consciousness of selflessness, for the element of individuality is inevitable. The fusion of selflessness can occur only where there is clear awareness of the future. Selflessness is not built on experience of the past. Only a real sense of the future can inform an inner assessment of the limits of the possible.

61. Qualities of action. If an action is small, it needs the support of various artificial things. When an action becomes great, it no longer requires these earthly things. This is the first touchstone of action.

The second quality of action is mobility. Like a whirlwind of primary matter, true action should quiver with possibility. Only flight can complete the manifestation of a light-bearing thought.

The third quality of action is unexpectedness. Every action that has struck the minds of others resulted from an unconventional manner of thinking.

The fourth quality of action is elusiveness. This quality alone protects action from disastrous attack.

The fifth quality of action is convincingness. As each bolt of lightning connects our consciousness with the Cosmos, so every action must strike like a glittering sword.

The sixth quality of action is legitimacy. Only an awareness of the fundamental principles of planetary evolution can translate action into something immutable.

The seventh quality of action is its pure execution. By this means, it is possible to move heavy objects without tiring. The impact of body and spirit should be understood equally; despite all that has said before, the impact of thought is still underestimated.

62. Qualities of expectation. The highest expectation is the expectation of the evolution of the World. Everyday expectations can be divided into dark, slumberous, and vigilant. The chaos of dark expectations only causes harm to space. Slumberous expectations are like smouldering embers. Vigilant expectations represent the readiness to accept something new at any hour.

The inner quality of expectation is its growth. With what can this characteristic be better combined than the evolution of the worlds? This expectation must penetrate our whole life. It should fill our work with the thrill of action, for this combination is the finest and the most beautiful.

Upon entering the house of the restless, say: "Expect the evolution of the World!"

63. We appreciate the thought that generates a decision. Decisions are evaluated by the quality of applicability. Applicability is judged by knowledge of spirit; then follows action which may evoke delight. After all, whoever delights also believes. Even faith must be grounded.

The Leader evaluates well and applies firmly. Should he be accused of calculation, he should not reject the claim, for calculation is opposed to madness, and madness is the opposite of knowledge of spirit. No matter what circle we choose, we always return to the great knowledge of spirit.

64. It is not words, but the filling of space that nudges the Leader towards an immutable order. The destruction of fear will help her at the difficult hour. It is especially hard to overcome the perception of loneliness. Wise tales often include the lone battle with the self. The fighter — also known as scout, adviser, decision-maker, and hero. Note that this word has almost been banished from the vocabulary of the old world. The hero becomes unacceptable in the lives of the small-hearted. Like a stranger, he would hang his head amidst their prosperity. Learn to be among heroes. The world will be stunned by the force of heroism.

Let children call themselves heroes and imitate the qualities of remarkable people. Let them be given books with clear expression that set out the precise contours of labour and will, without softening their depiction. If for nothing else but medicinal purposes, this cheerful call of life is irreplaceable. Such material should be provided as soon as possible. The few who are able to provide it must be protected.

65. Be wary of those that have no time. Above all, false busyness indicates an inability to use the treasures of time and space. This type is capable of performing primary forms of work only. It is impossible to involve them in creativity.

We have already spoken of the liars in cycles that steal other people's time; now let us speak of the petty idlers and feeble-minded who block life's path. They are busy, but like a vessel filled with pepper, their work always brings them bitterness. They are as pompous as turkey-cocks, for while counting the number of stinking clouds from their smoking, they offer a place for the workings of intoxication. They make up hundreds of excuses that fill the cracks of their rotten work. They cannot find a single hour for what is most urgent. In their stupidity they are willing to become impertinent and to forsake their very existence. They are as unfruitful as the thieves of time.

We know many hard-workers who will always find an hour for what is most important; they do not feel that they are busy. People who are generous with their labour will receive generously. This quality of assimilating the meaning of labour is essential to the expansion of consciousness. Is there anything that could possibly replace the joy that comes from expansion of consciousness?

66. Acquiescence is like a long-opened bottle of fragrance, while creative patience is like an old, sealed bottle of wine.

The Leader follows the intensity of creativity; in any social structure, where diverse creativity is taking wings, the structure is secure. When creativity is suffocating, it is a clear sign that there is an error in the structure. Such errors should not be permitted to fester. Summon the masons, and relay the walls until a song sounds freely.

The principle of freedom of approach, as well as the principle of freedom of service and labour, must be guarded. Onerousness experienced in the early stages of an endeavour is merely a sign of imperfection. Wisdom will be confirmed by the solid landmarks that surround the designated figure of knowledge.

We shall indicate right direction by opening the right door.

67. In the life of every cooperation a situation may arise in which development in a particular direction may harm the intended effect. In this case the Leader must find a path along new goals, broad enough to absorb any friction. Let us avoid calling this kind of friction competition or giving it an even worse name.

Just as in dangerous straits ships proceed one by one, in the development of cooperation there may be a need to divide the movement of participants. Instead of causing potential harm, this may well result in the mastering of new domains. When muscles acquire bulk, you should know how to channel the energy. If you do not prevent congested movement, discord will assuredly result.

A diversity of tasks is essential, as otherwise, the forces within a growing consciousness will collide. It is the Leader's responsibility not to allow useful forces to become a jar of scorpions. Fortunately, there are so many impending tasks that it is not difficult to find an urgent conquest upon which to lay one's forces.

Often growing strength is confused with antagonism. Often, instead of calmly taking advantage of an opportunity, the flames of hatred are fanned. The Leader must not fail to note this psychological moment and should assign a new task at just the right time.

Complications can be avoided by guaranteeing victory through highly practical methods. The Teaching of reality must conform to depth of complexity in the flow of evolution. The emergence of new world structures must be firmly protected.

68. You can train your consciousness to right understanding of the ownership of the things around you, for the consciousness is noble that says: "Nothing belongs to me, it belongs to us, and we are scattered all over the planet." Can anyone really be satisfied with a life of personal gain? Can one really appropriate for oneself the free primordial matter that imbues each object? Learn to sense the need for the presence of matter in each and every thing. Often people agree to acknowledge matter in the distant ether, but consider it ridiculous to acknowledge matter in human-made everyday objects. The recognition of high matter in every single object raises a person's perception of life in all its detail.

69. Modern industry and all material products are so unbalanced quantitatively and qualitatively that as yet they exclude the possibility of the proper distribution of things. Forced, unconscious distribution engenders cunning and falsehood. Should one await new opportunities in a state of inaction, or deepen the essence of consciousness? There is no point in forcibly taking things away, thereby creating a passion for junk. The important thing is to eradicate land ownership and the principle of inheritance and to reasonably carry out the educational task of communicating the degrading and egotistical significance of property. It is essential that this consciousness represent not a renunciation, but a free conquest. When without cunning people learn of the impracticality of ownership, a collective allied to the principle of cooperation will emerge.

70. The poisonous breath of the notion of *ownership* can be eliminated only by a well thought-out programme for schools. Similarly, religion is affirmed not by prohibition but through offering the Teaching of Life. There is no literature against the notion of *property*. As an item in a party manifesto it is unconvincing. Very few have defeated the dragon of junk. But many dream of making their own acquisitions. How just historical comparisons must be! With what discipline must biological details be gleaned in order to demonstrate the iniquity and futility of ownership. The laws and properties of matter are evidence that selfish ownership contradicts human nature.

71. Belief systems and laws preach against theft. Stealing is harmful as a concept, and reinforces the sense of ownership. Theft hinders the evolution of the world, and unenviable is the lot of those who harm world evolution. They set themselves back hugely.

What is significant is not that one object has passed from one pair of hands into another; what is significant is that two people then experience the fitful feeling of ownership.

The law on theft is imperfect, for the most significant theft — the theft of knowledge, ideas, and creativity — cannot be accounted for. One can only appreciate the treasure of time when one works for the Common Good. Least acceptable of all is to steal the time of one's brethren. Stealing time unthinkingly is tantamount to the theft of ideas.

72. Prohibition must be refuted; this is the law of aspiration. However, irreplaceable values should be guarded — for this, too, is the law of aspiration.

Let us look at things more directly — anything irreplaceable should be given priority in terms of preservation.

73. The Leader monitors the expediency of teaching in schools. For advanced pupils, there should be opportunities to progress further. If the swiftest ship must lower its sails for the sake of aligning ranks, would this not result in the killing of opportunity? Do you know how a ship's proportioned striving is created? And was it not built to cope with the greatest danger? How can you waste it on the transportation of frozen

vegetables? You should always preserve the opportunity for responsible advancement. Let slowness of step never hinder those who are able to proceed at a faster pace. Let the teacher vigilantly discern who can maintain the pace. There is no need to praise them, but their path should be cleared.

Intermediate courses should be created — then the quicker pupils will be able to run up them like steps. Do not conceal difficulties from them. For a certain type of consciousness, every heroic-like movement is light and joy. In addition, it is dependent upon the teacher to swiftly determine the direction of a pupil's thinking, as an erroneous instruction is a grave crime which may cost you your best workers. Every inflexible programme is a corpse which is beyond bearing beneath the sun of knowledge.

Schools should be strengthened as quickly as possible by examining the consciousness of their teachers. Create for teachers the best possible conditions so that you may entrust them with the responsibility of caring for the consciousness of younger workers. It is inconceivable that the schools of the future should resemble the cattle yards in which recent generations were mutilated. Fanaticism and prohibition should be replaced with opportunity.

Introduce the study of handicrafts, allow freedom of choice, and demand quality of labour. For this, every teacher must understand the importance of quality.

74. The Leader opposes prejudice and outmoded practices. With this awareness, she advises: "Treat the customs of others with care." Often foreign customs were built on a foundation of the development of knowledge in which case all accumulated debris should be washed away — but to demolish the significance of customs built on a rational foundation would be unjustified. If an architect sees that a foundation is firm, he will use it in a new building. There must be economy of resources on a world scale. The days of the luxury of destruction have vanished into the pages of history. The world is in need not of new elements, but of new combinations of existing elements. And the path of new conquerors is illumined not by the glowing of fires, but by sparks of energy that is newly attracted.

75. The art of thinking must be developed in schools. Every art requires practice. Likewise, thinking must be strengthened through exercise, yet this deepening should not be burdensome or boring, and therefore the instructor of the subject must be truly enlightened.

You can see that the most terrible calamities in the history of humanity have resulted from the inability to think. One can point to a multitude of examples in which short-sighted thinking and unbridled feeling have led entire peoples into the abyss. On the other hand, laziness and slowness of thinking have destroyed existing opportunities.

The Leader himself must provide an example of constant expansion of thinking so as to approach foresight. Of course, foresight results from communication with the Hierarchy. However, this Communication also depends on agility of thinking and clear aspiration.

The art of thinking should not be understood to be a kind of occult concentration. There is nothing of this sort in the art of thinking or the refinement of consciousness. Only a high degree of conscientiousness can establish the path of the thinker. At the same time, no one will say that the thinker is a special kind of person. Every child can be directed towards thinking. Thus, the art of thinking should be seen as pertaining to the health of the people.

Guidance of the masses obliges the Leader to expand individual consciousness.

76. The quality of the knowledge required should be defined. Knowledge must be unconditional. Any conditioned, restricted science causes irreparable harm. The free combination of elements leads to inimitable new achievements. Who would prescribe that a chemist confine herself to working with a single group of elements? Who would force a historian or a philosopher to avoid touching on historical fact? Who would order an artist to use but one colour? Knowledge is open to everything. The only advantages in fields of knowledge are great convincingness and attractiveness. If you want to captivate others with your knowledge, make it attractive — so attractive that the books of yesterday will appear as dry leaves. The victory of convincingness will relieve you of intolerable restrictions.

Most of all, concern yourself with the task of expelling similar restrictions from the lives of your pupils. This is particularly easy for the builders of a new life, for their book could be especially inspiring and engaging. Of course, a purely scripted exposition is unbearable. The miserable pharmacist will brush off anyone who cannot tolerate his untalented attitude to beauty. Inspiration should be allied to construction.

Plants reach up towards the Light — this is the immutable sign of all emerging consciousness. Follow the path of immutability and build life. There is nothing abstract in life, and life absorbs our every thought. Therefore, let us be realists in terms of the true reality.

77. Schools should teach respect for the articulation of concept. After all, parrots can mindlessly redirect concepts through space, often concepts of great significance. But people must understand that every word they pronounce has the power of a thunder-bearing arrow; words are the pedals of thought. The loss of the true meaning of original concepts has contributed much to contemporary savagery. People strew pearls before them like sand. Indeed, it is high time that many definitions be replaced.

Special courses should be established in schools: the concept of *spirit* should be explained in conjunction with physiology. Finally, knowledge should build a scientific bridge of aspiration to the spiritual. The New World will affirm a bold cognitive approach. Images of the Teachers will enter life as Friends. The Precept of the Teacher will sit on the shelf alongside other favourite titles.

78. You often talk about the imperfection of existing books. I would go a step further and say: the errors in these books are a heinous crime. Falsehood printed in books should be prosecuted as a grave form of slander. The falsehood of orators is prosecuted according to the number of listeners. The falsehood of authors is prosecuted according to the number of copies printed. It is a grave crime to fill people's libraries with lies. One must be able to sense the true intention of a writer in order to evaluate the significance of their mistakes. Ignorance will be the worst criteria. Next, fear and meanness. All these traits are inadmissible. They must be eliminated in the building of the new life. Prohibitive measures are always inappropriate. However, once an error has been discovered in a book, it should be removed. The need for the edit and the reprinting of the book should serve to bring the author to their senses. Every citizen has the right to expose a mistake. Of course, new views and thinking must not be hindered, but nor should incorrect data be allowed to mislead. Therefore, the responsibility to protect knowledge falls on all members of society. Books must be examined no later than within a year of publication; otherwise, the number of victims may be great indeed.

It is especially necessary to safeguard a book when its true merit is attacked. Entire abscesses of falsehood inhabit our library shelves. It would be unacceptable to preserve such parasites. You could put it like this — you can sleep in a bad bed, but never offer someone an inveracious book.

Why turn the best corner of the hearth into a lying buffoon? Books of this kind pollute the consciousness of children. The issue of books must be properly noted.

79. The laws of human perturbation cannot be determined by the logical breaking down of things into their obvious elements. How then can the knots in the thinking apparatus be untied without studying all the surrounding processes? Somewhere there is a sudden blaze of pink rays and the planned uprising of a whole people is stilled. Somewhere the currents of the ocean change, initiating a shift in world trade. These are obvious, coarse examples. But O how many subtle causes and effects permeate space and run furrows through the layers of humanity!

O you who decide the destiny of others, enter the laboratory and come up into the observatory. Even if you do not immediately find an analogy to the social problems that concern you, your inquisitive mind will grasp the complexity of the structure of reality. It will grasp the inseparability of individual destinies and the evolution of humanity from cosmic processes. Hence real knowledge devoid of prejudice is the true guide to the future. After all, anyone who isolates the science of human society from global processes, in effect cuts their own legs out from underneath them and condemns themselves to a cripple's existence.

80. Few attempts have been made to connect technology and the psyche. The Leader knows that a scientific approach towards the psyche eases all aspects of existence, and she will pay urgent attention to the capabilities of the psychic apparatus.

Psycho-technology would be a more accurate definition of the application of psychic energy.

It is interesting to note experiments with factory labour. Every experienced worker knows that machines require rest. It is difficult to give this phenomenon a more precise definition, but it is quite familiar even to those who know nothing of psycho-technology. We had the opportunity to conduct experiments in textile factories, where hundreds of looms were being operated by up to one hundred fairly skilled workers. The machines demanded rest outside of the standard period and regardless of the weaver's level of experience. After carrying out psychic tests on the weavers, it could be clearly seen that, in the hands of those weavers who possessed psychic energy, the looms required less rest, as though a living current were being imparted to the machine prolonging its vitality.

This living cooperation between worker and machine should be applied in labour communities. This beneficial condition can be achieved through the application of psycho-technology. The task of the state is to provide the most productive conditions possible, to take measures and focus the efforts of scientists on improving the life of the collective.

81. Should one renounce or multiply? Of course one should multiply exuberantly and joyfully, but only for the Common Good. The slightest hint of sectarianism or hypocritical limitation will contradict solar evolution. Austere joy evades the darkness.

The moles of suppression and restriction will never see the sun. Human consciousness is capable of absorbing slavish obsequiousness to such a degree that any new piece of knowledge will appear either a crime or madness. Is reality really to endure such base limitations?

82. The discipline of will and the command of consciousness has been discussed many times. The principle of vigorous responsibility has long been established; now we must be alert to the need to eradicate the narrowness of sectarianism and superstition. Sectarians dream of seizing power and subduing everything to their own rigid consciousness. The superstitious are most afraid of triggering a portent for someone by some accidental movement of their own and think about themselves far too much. Superstition and sectarianism are indicators of a very low level of consciousness. In those unfamiliar with the principle of assimilation, the potential for creativity is miniscule.

Superstition and sectarianism should be uncovered in every way possible. Do not hesitate to discuss these matters, for in doing so you destroy falsehood and fear.

Superstition can be eradicated only by venerating forces innate to human beings.

83. Cooperation is a repository for all potentialities and diverse experiences. Anyone who disparages the limits and power of cooperation is a traitor. Cooperation is the chalice of solar joy!

84. One should pay attention to the initial stages of epidemics. The manifestation of one or another mass disease impacts the collective strength of consciousness. The poisoning penetrates deeper than people realize; it regenerates and creates new microbes. Physical and psychic epidemics are highly pernicious. Such regenerated microbes can lead to the degeneration of entire family lines.

85. Some insects and reptiles choose to perish, as long as they can bite and release their venom. In the same way, the servants of darkness are willing to suffer the most unpleasant consequences, as long as they can create poisonous evil. These evil-doers, those who sometimes will even sacrifice themselves for villainy, should never be forgotten. One may point to many examples in which the evil plotted was of no benefit to the villain himself, and was nonetheless carried out by him due to the influence of dark forces.

The tricks employed by dark forces must be exposed. For example, there are certain places where one may find the corpses of humans and animals. The dark ones are aware that decomposition is required in order to attract the forces of the lowest spheres, and so they inventively arrange such hotbeds of turmoil and decomposition. For this reason, I long ago advised not keeping putrid meat, decaying plants, or foul water in the home. Rarely do people pay attention to such facts, despite their being confirmed by contemporary physicians.

86. You must stand constantly at the threshold of the future. You are new in every moment. You must not become fixated on the past, for it no longer exists. You can know the past, but unfortunate is any who attempts to apply the measures of the past.

The Leader is advised to remember that the past is incompatible with the future. The wisdom of perceiving fresh combinations is what unites the past with the future. It is not easy to hold the awareness constantly and courageously that worlds are renewed in every new instant, and yet from this source one may find an inexhaustible vigour. The Leader may assemble a Counsel of the Wise but let the Counsel be closed to those who are senile in spirit or who stand with their face turned to the past. The light of the future is the Light of the Hierarchy.

87. The Leader must affirm good deeds in the consciousness of the people. All means of spreading messages about the good must be at his disposal. Any silence on the Leader's part will become filled with the evil that pursues every deviation from the good. One must acknowledge these shifts in foundations so as to be on constant guard; the Leader communicates with his people like a father. In this way one may restore the harmony of worlds.

88. Of course, the elder-masters, as well as the Altai Sisters and Teachers of different schools of knowledge, the arts, and crafts represent a mobile host of enlightenment. It is in these individuals that local teachers will find the best companions. It is they who will ignite the fires of delight and inspiration. Even those local teachers who apply every possible diligence in teaching their subject, still bear the yoke of the mundane.

They will happily welcome a guest mentor. The very unexpectedness of their arrival represents a manifestation of the unusual to which hearts are so drawn. Itinerant teachers themselves enjoy a wonderful diversity that renews and multiplies their strength. The Leader herself may sometimes participate in these light-bearing pilgrimages. Of course, often it is the participating students who later come into the Dwelling of the Elders and the Sisters. Life must be good in their Dwellings. In this way it is possible to create true spiritual centres of labour and enlightenment. Let knowledge be affirmed through the most heartfelt and engaging measures.

89. The Leader must participate personally in the Council of Publishers. The Council should consist of publishing house representatives. It is they who oversee the expulsion of vulgarity and falsehood. Those who are thrice proven guilty of these crimes are deprived of the right to publish. In addition the Council itself oversees the attractive appearance of publications and works to keep prices affordable. They also see to it that a great number of useful leaflets are distributed fully among the reading public. Let even the wrapping paper contain useful advice. Of course, publishers should form a Cooperative.

90. Corruptibility must be eradicated at all cost, but one should not rely on punitive measures which are of little use; in school ethics lessons, the notion should be affirmed that corruptibility runs contrary to the dignity of human beings. Of course, Cooperatives should expel from their staff anyone with dealings in corruption. The Leader himself must be highly attentive to any indication or sign of such decay.

Along with corruption, no less shameful is dereliction of duty. However, this crime is so absorbed at an early age that an impact can be made only on individuals in infancy.

Let children become accustomed to the work of adults. With quality of labour comes the realization of duty. Any case of negligence, forgetfulness, or evasiveness can be eradicated only in one's own heart.

91. Fear is incompatible with the concept of *Leader*. Every demonstration of fear in and of itself destroys some portion of respect for the Leader. She should not express confusion or distraction. Fear compels even the intelligent to increase their personal security. Yet the Leader does not need guards. She may instead be surrounded by colleagues and assistants.

The phenomenon of fear has ruined many states. *Horror* is a most contagious notion. Just imagine: once the Leader becomes infected with horror, can one really picture her in communication with the Hierarchy? Nations are sensitized to anything of which they themselves are guilty, above all, of course, to fear. Nations will respect courage, even in the strangest of forms. But, fear and indecision will not be forgiven; besides, every manifestation of fear severs the silver thread.

92. Courage may remain within the seed and never reveal itself in the form of light-bearing armour. But when our consciousness is entirely transferred to a domain free of fear and despondency, then we are invulnerable to impurity. We must understand where our fortress lies, and to hasten there without deviating from the path. In this way, courage can be strengthened.

93. The Leader never assembles all his forces in one place — this is one of the main factors of his invincibility. However, not only are the forces of the Leader spread among different places, sometimes they are moved about in response to an order that depends on him alone. People are sometimes aware of the relocation of forces, yet they are equally aware that much happens without their knowledge. Thus the movements of Leader's forces should not be revealed to the public.

At the same time it is well known that, while gases are not used, there are certain rays which can operate without fail. Also, it is impossible to hide the fact that psychic energy offers much greater protection than gases can. However, the use of these energies is in the hands of trusted parties only. Any risk of betrayal on their part may be excluded, for the same energy can have the reverse effect.

Thus, the protection of the Leader takes on a completely new aspect. Let us not forget that, of course, warnings of danger are given via communication with the Hierarchy. Forces of psychic energy are the most dependable armour; people mistakenly use the incongruous word *intuition*, where what is really being referred to is supreme knowledge of the heart.

94. The Leader must guard herself against the potential revocation of her own decrees. Such irresolution would lead to the same miseries as displays of fear. The subsequent loss of respect for her would be irreparable; hence the Leader must not hope that a mistake made today may be corrected tomorrow. Mistakes must not be made. The passing of a decree may be held off, but once passed, the decree is law.

95. Usually people are mistaken when, due to their limited consciousness, they assume that an object can exist only in one form. They struggle to imagine that in ancient times people were able to work with all kinds of energies but that they applied them quite differently. People also forget that when they move home, they themselves destroy all sorts of things they no longer find necessary; in the same way, wise Teachers take measures to conceal in a timely manner what must not be shared prematurely. Can new discoveries really be revealed ahead of time? Their foundation might easily be shaken by such self-willed attempts. For does not the Hierarchy participate in discoveries? Do you not know that We destroyed many discoveries that would have been harmful on account of their untimeliness? Remember that the Guiding Hand knows no rest as it watches over the conduit of opportunities for Good.

96. Indeed, the new structure must be devoid of luxury, all the more so since luxury corresponds to neither beauty nor knowledge. However, the boundaries of luxury are winding and cannot be defined by a single law. The Leader must take upon himself this heavy duty, too. He is capable of utterly destroying all vulgarity that is the companion of luxury. The Leader may listen to the opinion of the best experts, but ultimately the decision should rest with him.

97. To develop a perception of beauty, the study of the beauty of life should be established in schools. The history of arts and knowledge should form part of this subject, for it must not only touch on former conceptions, but also contain guidelines for contemporary achievements. The teacher of this subject must be truly educated in order to avoid bigotry, which carries within it the seed of ignorance.

98. The World lives by Mystery. As the Supreme Mystery is unrevealable, so in every manifestation of tension there is an element of mystery. People discern in their hearts the boundaries of this mystery and are able to respect them. Mysteries should not be invented, they should be revered — herein lies the justification of the human personality. The essence of the Leader's intentions is a mystery, but the manifestation of her actions is seen in the good of the people.

99. Can we really expect that the distorted budgets of the State can be balanced without the need for special measures? Issuing bank notes and loans will not help, but, instead, drive the illness within. Attention should be paid to the proper distribution of the population and its forces. Monstrous cities, abscesses of debauchery and disease, must be spread out more evenly, if the equilibrium is not to be disturbed. The confluence of crowds with deserts alongside must not be allowed to shake the foundations of life. Living in Nature should become an accessible and attractive prospect.

State-of-the-art discoveries make it possible to integrate cultural achievements even in remote locations. When schools explain the meaning of life as being self-improvement, the flow of people wanting to live in Nature will increase. Also cooperatives will provide the opportunity to return to finest-quality domestic production. The same cooperatives will help the State maintain a balanced budget. The cooperative phenomenon will enable the State to assign to them a significant portion of its expenses, for example: the maintenance of communication lines, forestry and water sectors, health care industry, homeland security provision, in addition to many other items that cooperatives require. Of course, schools and entertainment facilities should be supported by cooperatives under the supervision of the State.

In addition, cooperatives, by their very nature, benefit society through indirect taxation. Any direct poll tax should not be allowed to become sizeable, as such a circumstance will always cause discontent. On the other hand, indirect taxes can accrue from such a multitude of things that they are no longer visible to the eye. The network of cooperatives should cover all areas of the State and, rather than requiring a large number of employees, they should require minimal supervision. The Council of the Supreme Economy should be led by the Leader himself. Thus the building of the entire State is constructed with one Peak.

100. Every conversation with the Leader should give encouragement. There is no place for threat or derogation. Everyone, even lower-ranked employees, can be supported in their best qualities. Even adolescents can contribute useful ideas; indeed, the human heart always delights when it feels that its best qualities are appreciated.

101. To those who cannot grasp the idea of *Leader*, we say: your every word presupposes the priority of something or someone. You may not notice that each of your assertions is based on a discovery of something made by someone. There is not a single human being that does not have the need of a teacher. Only do not let feelings of superiority enter your heart. The understanding of the Hierarchy will help establish the phenomenon of *Leader* as one who, in relation to the Higher Beings, is not Leader but follower.

People who are influenced by ignorance sometimes try to cut through the tow ropes, yet every sailor will tell you that masts are chopped down when the elements overpower human strength. The same sailor knows that without masts and ropes any voyage is doomed. Hence the education system should affirm the notion of the absolute necessity of a Hierarchy throughout the Universe.

102. Every inventor and scientist must feel that their discoveries will be protected by the State. There is no need for scientists to waste their efforts on safeguarding their findings; the State itself must take upon itself both the matter of protection and the broad application of useful discoveries. Inventors must be rewarded by the State and afforded favourable conditions for the continuation and development of their work. It is unacceptable for creative forces to be burdened with the formalities of stupidity. The Leader herself must be aware of where the creative forces of the people are directed. Thus, the contribution of labour by those who improve quality of life will be fairly valued.

103. Class, as a criterion of convention, cannot be allowed to exist in the New World. The military class should be transformed into a common defence force, which works decisively for the protection of all. Essential defence methods should be taught in school.

104. Verbal commands remain essential to life, even if humanity does have thousands of written languages at its disposal. There are three reasons for this: first, a command is not always subject to written representation; second, people pay less attention when they rely on writing; third, Supreme Precepts are never written down; thus lips utter the Highest Orders, one heart to another.

In the same way, the Leader preserves the Lord's Commands in his heart and, in turn, gives the resulting order verbally. This simple consideration still deserves specific mention, for anyone that does not know the Hierarchy will not understand the holiness of the Command. Many instructions regarding the laws of Nature are required in order to understand the full beauty of the law of attraction, which underpins the Hierarchy's foundation. The ignorant do not realize just where slavery and freedom lie — the former in darkness, the latter in the Light of the Hierarchy.

105. Torture and violence can be eliminated once and for all. There is no need for such dark measures where the knowledge of psychic energy prevails. The Court marks on film the internal state of the accused. Confessions should be verified by a clairvoyant. The accused himself will speak the truth by a command which cannot be disobeyed by any will, no matter how strong. In this manner psychic energy will come into focus. Of course, the new science of the celestial bodies will help in explaining Truth.

106. Indeed, respect for spirit can only grow. We must eradicate godlessness. The fact is that it is better to preserve fragments of awareness of the Hierarchy, even in tentative forms, than to return to the abyss of chaos.

When people first heard of the inaccessibility of the Supreme, they began to overthrow all that is invisible. This is why, by My Command, godlessness will be prosecuted, for it has taken the form of overt satanism.

107. The death penalty should be abolished, for the annihilation of robbers in battle is not punishment. A multitude of criminals will turn to labour by the force of suggestion. Just as drunkenness and other vices, so diseases of criminality may be cured by command of the will. Also, it is worth remembering that many crimes are committed under the influence of possession. Such people should be given treatment, rather than punished. Of course, intense systematic labour is a decisive factor in this kind of treatment. Possessors hate any kind of labour. They will attempt to plunge the individual into chaos, but the essence of labour is a manifestation to the contrary.

There is no use in pondering where these strong suggestions come from; they are many but they are scattered. When the Institute of Psychic Energy is established, it will bring together many helpful colleagues. Remember that the Institute of Astrology will serve as a close assistant in the verification of data. It was not long ago that governments were ashamed to speak of celestial bodies as well as human powers, and yet enlightened individuals must focus on the phenomenon of psychic energy.

108. The Leader must always be of buoyant disposition, so that no one should ever pick up emanations of despondency. But such vigour can be achieved only when devotion to the Hierarchy is strong, when communication with it has entered the heart. The same Source creates amicability, too, which can open the most troublesome of doors. The Leader must keep before her the Image of the Hierarch so as to find grounds for amicability in every case. She must be acquainted with the Archangel's Fiery Sword in order to be capable of discerning the boundaries of justice. Who can say when all demonstrations of amicability have been exhausted? The Hierarch alone is able to take it upon Himself to arrive at such a decision. The most peaceful selfless Hero is one such example of this.

109. The Leader perceives periods of everyday work as moments of eternity. He can never become exhausted, even when faced with the slowness of evolution. Human clocks show a lot of time, but where the Leader dwells the measurements are different; therefore, he must be able to offer kindly help both to those who lag behind and to those who forge ahead.

Only communication with the Hierarchy can give the Leader the measures of Three Worlds. From this Source comes the Leader's freedom from fatigue. The human mind cannot sustain eternal labour — only the inexhaustible Power of the Hierarchy can send strengthening rays and enable one to comprehend the true meaning of labour. Without the Hierarchy, the Leader is merely a blade of grass caught up in a whirlwind. Collecting rays of the Fiery World means forging one's own armour.

110. In agriculture, as in trades and in creativity, the personality must be developed. Cooperatives serve to encourage such development, but by no means to enslave. Enslavement and negation of personality can be seen only in unintelligent forms of cooperation.

As an executioner does not know the thoughts of the heads he cuts off, so ignorant individuals who imagine themselves to be cooperators destroy powers of creativity. Just as executioners have always been despised, so too, will the executioners of thoughts be despised. Ascent and not humiliation will resound in the appeals of the Leader. The very presence of the Leader is a symbol of the invocation of the power of the people.

111. The Leader may meet with members of the younger generation, for whom her every appearance will be a celebration. She will suggest fascinating projects, point out how even the little ones can be of use to the State, and will recognize and appreciate every sign of heroism. The Leader herself will record the names of the little heroes, for heroism is embedded in their spirit. Never has a coward consciously become a hero. Heroes should be marked out even among those of school years and the fire of selflessness supported. No one takes note of how the main characteristics of human nature are expressed. Too often people have humiliated the most valuable signs of promise.

Above all the New Era will be quick to recognize and safeguard the strengths of the people.

112. The Leader must not appoint embittered individuals to positions of responsibility. This trait must be avoided at all costs, for embitterment is a limitation. Of course, to a certain extent, a limitation can be cured, as can bitterness. Both qualities are amenable to suggestion, but such a transfiguration requires time. Terrible harm is spawned by bitterness; like an insurmountable obstacle, it tumbles down upon all the actions of those who have succumbed to resentment.

113. The Leader is never born into a time of slumber; days of aspiration and days of burden create the Leader. As a symbol of movement, he leads the people into a fruitful land. Wherever the Leader has been sent, there the Promised Land is already evident. Thus, the appearance of the Leader is a good sign, a sign of prosperity, a sign of departing from burial and nearing the Light. So let us never regret times of slumber, even when there is nowhere to be led. The Leader should convey to the people the energy which is essentially given by the Hierarchy of Light. The Leader will not utter a word of prohibition; wherever the destined gates are, the people will find the solution to their needs; and this will be no empty promise, for the Hierarchy knows no emptiness. And let us give thanks when, instead of a time of slumber, we are given the dawn.

114. The Leader gathers her colleagues through a series of tests. First of all, she will ask the one being tested to describe a circumstance of their choosing. If the communication starts with the negation of something, this is a sign that the colleague is unsuitable, for there is something meaningful to be found in everything. There is a special eye that will discern every good seed that exists. It is important to choose such far-sighted

colleagues. The Leader must not yield to the temptation of negation.

115. Mendicancy is totally inadmissible. Each cooperative should ensure that there is enough work for everyone in its field. Only the infirm should need to populate the House of Mercy, but there are very few so feeble as to be completely deprived of work. The diversity of labour is inexhaustible; one need only have the resourcefulness to discover one's capacity for work.

116. The Leader takes care to move his employees around in an expedient way or to maintain their usefulness in the same place. It is impossible to establish standard time-frames — everything depends on expediency.

117. The Leader must always hold before her the ultimate goal. Many undertakings have been confounded purely by losing sight of the main goal. Everyday life has erased the fulfilment of God-given tasks, and human-set tasks have multiplied, burying one's cosmic purpose. One must understand that only communication with the Hierarchy can support the spirit in rising above mundanity. It is impossible to avoid the details of daily life, but they can be covered with rainbow rays of spirit. May the Leader always remember that the main goal is the self-improvement of the people and collective awareness of the treasures of the Three Worlds.

118. One must avoid prohibitions of any kind and replace them with an Edict issued in a timely manner. It sounds much better for the Leader to say: "Do this and create," than "I disallow." Every negation eradicates a portion of the people's respect for the Leader; indeed, Edicts are effective only in proportion to their timeliness. Yet who, except the Hierarch, is able to discern timeliness? Therefore, the pearl of the Leader's power lies only in communication with the Hierarch. It is impossible to melt such a pearl, for it will emit poison in the process of decomposition. One must guard the pearl as a single irreplaceable treasure. If the Leader should reject the Communication, he will instantly become the most ordinary of people, and the torn thread will cast him far back into the past.

119. One can recognize the Supreme Power when its action is mutual, like in a resultant sum. The concept of reciprocity is essential; a shield can appear only through the combination of different forces. However, the Leader must always direct her heart as though the Hierarch were standing next to her.

120. An awareness of the Supreme Powers is not to be found in school, or in the external, but abiding right in the heart, as the most fundamental memory of life in the Subtle World. We might say: be blessed, you who have preserved the most Beautiful in your heart. Humanity's thunderclouds occur when we forget what is most essential. Night is given as the elevation of the spirit, yet in their ignorance people have been known to compare sleep to death. It is absurd to compare such a wonderful mystery to decomposition. One should instil the idea from an early age that sleep is referred to as a conversation with the Angels. When words become unnecessary, comprehension through the heart begins.

121. Supervision must be highly vigilant, yet it should not be interpreted as a sign of distrust. Supervision should be transformed into cooperation and mutual enquiry. Measures of trust and thoroughness in quality must be carried out from top to bottom. A multitude of useful activities have been discredited and eliminated simply as a result of a general hatred for supervision.

Of course, the cause of such inexpediency will be ignorance; when people gain insight into the Subtle and Fiery Worlds, they will realize the boundlessness of relationships. Indeed, who can exist outside the Hierarchy?! Only ignoramuses or conscious deceivers, under different conspiratorial names, can darken the Hierarchy. And they would deliver not the freedom of the Hierarchy, but the stigma of slavery.

The Leader must cleanse the people from any stain of slavery. From an early age one must repeatedly assert the freedom of the discipline of spirit. Dignity and honour of any kind can be awakened. After all, without honour, people cannot be honest. One should not imagine that slavery could ever be approved by the Hierarchy. On the contrary, the Fiery World seeks colleagues, not slaves. Consider refining the heart a measure of honour. Thus let us not forget that it is in the most everyday situations that the foundations of the world's grandeur are laid.

122. To read a book is not the same as to comprehend it. The Leader must understand to what extent his colleagues are actually imbued with the harmonious creation of the state. No one can refuse to take part in the work as long as it is within their power to do so. Though it is possible to possess more, or less human knowledge, those who work for the people must be distinguished by a genuine willingness to labour for the common good.

123. One should demonstrate one's care for the Hierarchy. The Hierarchy is not a superior authority, but the Stronghold of Love. Only from love is the kind of reverence born that would create discipline. However, few love those who help them — which means that ignorance is great!

124. What should you do if, upon entering a house, you notice a viper on your host's table? Should you ponder the matter up until such time as the snake kills your friend, or will you destroy it immediately? We say: save your dear one from evil. Do not cloud your head with confusion; take action for the greater good. It is impossible to weigh a viper and a human being on the same pair of scales. It is impossible to equate the lowest consciousness with the very temple of consciousness. If we cease to discriminate, what will remain of our responsibility before the world? Whoever saves a snake to lose a friend is no hero. Whoever evades their duty, trying to find words of apology, is no hero. Whoever fails to understand the difference between the greater and the lesser is no hero. Whoever has lost the yardstick of the heart is no hero. The Leader knows the measure of the heart as well as the fiery decision.

125. Indeed, the Leader will not only talk to the people, but her edicts will also be published in newspapers and widely broadcasted on the radio. Not so much having personal conversations as producing printed notifications and, most importantly, radio broadcasts.

The voice of the Leader must be heard in many solitary and distant places. She must show that all creation is close to her and that anyone striving for the improvement and enhancement of life will meet with encouragement and affection on the part of the Leader. Balancing the principles of life must meet with fair treatment, starting from above. No one should feel that there is a partition wall between themselves and the Leader. The emergence of fresh ideas — a creative establishment or discovery — must be announced by local cooperatives and reach the Leader with lightning speed. She, of course, has other Hierarchical resources at her disposal that will acquaint her with all important news.

126. The most powerful Avatars do not bear within themselves any earthly distinctions, but affirm themselves through the manifestation of spiritual creativity. You should not be surprised to hear that strong spirits are never fully recognized by their contemporaries — this is how it should be, for their measures correspond to the future, when a code of laws is made for one portion of the approach to the next rung of life.

Accept that people will never be able to admit that the highest achievement is in the development of the heart. Cooperation and living in community are based on the heart. People fail to realize this simple truth. Mechanization hinders them from finding significant routes into the Fiery World.

127. Some metals are easily connected, while others repel each other — the Leader himself must observe these lines of good and evil. Both sides create whole connected chains. But the main obstacle faced by the State consists in the mechanical mixing of opposite principles, which leads to premature decomposition. The heart — as well as communication with the Hierarchy — will tell you where the connectable parts lie. Human beings need the balance of heart and mind. Cooperation confirms equilibrium. The sacred number of Pythagoras is the balance of beauty. Much of this axiom has been made inapplicable to the present. It is an onerous task — communicating with people about balance.

128. *Competition* is one of the most difficult concepts. Only the fiery heart can understand what measures may be placed either on the side of the light or the dark. Competition is approved by the Leader herself. The pure understanding of development produces competition. But wherever there is wild and unbridled consciousness, competition will lead to mutual destruction. Envy nestles around competition and can lead to the most cunning crimes.

Cooperation must counteract competition that is so poorly understood. It is not easy to discern the limits of reasonable competition. The very word *competition* is dangerous, for it hints at jealousy — or in other words, a distorted notion of allegiance. Therefore, where possible, it is better to replace the concept of *competition* with that of *self-improvement*.

The current interpretation of a multitude of concepts must be revised. One has to acknowledge that an accurate history of belief systems would reveal the roots of many highly distorted concepts. Care must be taken to ensure that the language of fundamental concepts is as sonorous and as defining as possible.

129. A language may be enriched by new definitions, but there is no benefit in a senseless whistle. The sound of each letter denotes the vibration of certain energy centres. It is absurd to disturb such consonance without good reason. Pay attention to the sounds of ancient place names; newer variants do not always produce the same beneficial vibration. Ancient place names had meanings rooted in the dawn of time. Often no amount of philology is enough to find the root meaning embedded by powerful peoples of the past. Hence, we are all the more obliged to treat our inheritance with the utmost care — an inheritance unknown, yet one which compels our hearts to resound.

130. One may observe how furiously people now object to the concept of *Leader*, and yet at the same time ardently await one. It is instructive to note the discrepancy between the processes of the brain and the heart. The brain follows conventional thinking and repeats well-known formulas. However, the heart, even one which is weak and unbalanced, preserves grains of Truth. Where the brain feels strengthened through negation, the heart, albeit timidly, still trembles with joy at the prospect of an emerging solution. People who raise objections against constructive endeavours usually have nothing to offer in return. Yet it is these objectors who will be found among the first to follow the Leader. They may whisper in disagreement, but they will execute an Edict to the letter. They will ultimately accept the Hierarchy — not only because of their slavish nature, but on account of the workings of the heart, which will point out to them that in moments of danger they should keep their balance and remain close to a powerful authority figure. Hence the Leader should not be perturbed by the voices of ghosts.

131. Why so many tests, if the heart is capable of creating a spiritual transformation? The answer is simple: the heart has been neglected, no longer applied to life. Thus many are obliged to improve their consciousness through a trial period. When you hire a servant, you either trust their eyes or you assign them a test. In the same way, the heart of another may convincingly appeal to your gaze, while your mind likens their eyes to small tin bowls. Whenever possible, advise seekers to follow the path illumined by the radiance befalling their gaze.

132. The Leader must clearly determine with whom she can work. However, once a choice of colleagues has been made, one should refrain from reminding them of their past. Anything could have happened in the past! It is the past that prevents one from turning wholly to the future — many a petty earthly stone of the past hinders one from continuing along the urgent path of the present! Yet one must become accustomed to the urgent path, for none other exists. Many are the suffering and unfortunate that count every second as they await help. Shall we really not make haste?

133. One must be able to strictly differentiate between what represents a contradiction and what represents a special working method. If a left-handed person is able to create with his left hand, the meaning of his achievements will not contradict the work of his right hand. But people are constrained by conventional measures, and even now they fail to understand wherein the value of labour consists; any unfamiliar method tends to arouse suspicion.

What a disgusting feeling suspicion is! Suspicion has nothing in common with the Fiery World. A fit of suspicion makes a person worse than an animal; the latter at least retains its instinct, while suspicion corrodes all the senses. Of course, suspicion is a vestige from the darkest times. Fortunately, it is susceptible to healing by suggestion, but such an infection should not be allowed to fester in the first place.

134. The Leader himself should be able to bring the people's consciousness closer to the measures of the highest. The character of the entire country depends on the Leader — he is the exponent of its potential. The people will only revere a Leader who is the exponent of the nation's true treasures. The Leader should sense where these treasures are to be found; he will also come to know from where he can expect a hostile attack. Not a single day goes by that the dark forces do not attempt to wreak destruction. However, everyone should be able to fathom where lies destruction and where lies renewal.

135. Indeed, cruelty must be eradicated, not only cruelty of action but cruelty of thought, too, of which the latter is worse than the former. Government measures should be aimed at suppressing any inclination towards cruelty from infancy. As the most inhuman, dim, and spiteful darkness, the leprosy of base thinking must be cleansed.

Children are not cruel until they see a cruel action for the first time, which undoubtedly unleashes a torrent of dark chaos. Only a handful are able to resist independently the stream of darkness — such an achievement of consciousness is rare indeed. The Leader cannot assume this accomplishment of everyone; on the contrary, she should take measures geared towards the very lowest level. Also, let us not repeat numbly the great commandment, "Thou shalt not kill," but instead ponder where the greater amount of killing takes place — in hand, in word, or in thought? One should take into account that people's thinking is ready to murder.

136. You yourself know that the soundest path is the path of amicability. Let us recall what dangers we have avoided thanks to amicability! Perhaps, we are unaware of the limits and full dimensions of such dangers, yet our heart will testify that it is amicability that has helped us through our darkest hours.

137. The Leader must not always be expected to make an immediate decision — it is another thing to hear his opinion. He is able to sense the underlying cause of events. Such heart knowledge can be developed through observation. The ability to distinguish the primary circumstance and singular understanding of what is most necessary is key to reaching a decision.

The power of observation is nothing miraculous; it is born of respect for all that exists. Of course, the Leader must possess the power of observation, for today's joy may be tomorrow's grief, and vice versa. But the task of perceiving with the heart is an engaging one, sensing wherein lies the leading condition? Usually the ebb and flow of energy is mirrored in the face of others. Poor is the Leader who fails to notice the wave moving beneath lived experience. For people normally see only what is happening in their own consciousness. The Leader must not allow these transient shadows to cloud her own consciousness.

138. The nature of things must be taught among other key subjects. It must be beautifully told in all its actuality. Knowledge of the continuity of worlds must be presented complete with scientific comparisons. Religion will not contradict this presentation of the subject; on the contrary, it will help by virtue of its most ancient insights.

The subject of the nature of things will serve as the threshold to a comprehension of Living Ethics. One must discover why honour, dignity, and all the other qualities of humanity are essential. From their earliest years children must learn about the Subtle and Fiery Worlds; they must understand the principle of the Hierarchy and the Good. The sooner they are reminded of the Hierarchy and other Truths, the easier it will be for them to recall their former knowledge.

The Hierarchy will serve as the basis that purifies the concept of *God* in all its grandeur. Only thus will the concept of the Supreme cease to be perceived as a mere abstraction and become merged with all facets of Existence. It is necessary that the Leader and the government should understand how comprehension of the Supreme Idea can be improved. Schools should validate all the attractiveness of Existence in its full grandeur.

139. Danger lies in accumulating vibrations of tension. People are constantly surrounded by a multitude of dangers, but notice very few of them. When the Leader says, "Live in danger," she could also be saying, "Observe the dangers and thereby succeed." It is impossible to live apart from danger altogether, but it is a wonderful thing to turn dangers into a carpet of heroic deeds. The Leader is aware that she is carrying out a mission in which dangers will serve only as drivers — as such the Leader does not dwell on danger. The very thought of danger can be harmful. In thinking about danger, we intensify its vibration which can destroy our own balance.

Preserving strength should not be confused with fear or perplexity. We should be vigilant and cautious for the sake of accomplishing our mission in the best possible manner. Yet we cannot allow danger to burden the focus of our awareness. The Teacher must first and foremost insist upon the liberation of his disciple from the phantom of danger. The disciple must always hold himself to the standard of not spending a single drop of his higher energy without purpose. Thinking about danger affects many of our energy centres and chaotically consumes what valuable energy we have. Thinking about danger even affects the quality of a person's pulse, yet the desire to better accomplish one's mission strengthens the heart. And so, let us act as efficiently as possible.

140. Upon entering a monastic order, the individual was usually alerted to the difficulties associated with such a path. Some will say, "It is easy"; others will warn, "It is very difficult." To people with fiery hearts you can say: "It is easy"; but to those with an ordinary consciousness it would be more appropriate to warn: "It is very difficult." If a person runs away from a single warning of the difficulties, they will not be suited to the persistent labour involved. One should not gather those who are known to be unsuitable to the task. Fear of work is itself a form of betrayal.

141. Alexandrian philosophers used to say: "Do not condemn the World, for it was created by Great Thought!" It is not Creation that is at fault but our judgement of it. We can accumulate thoughts of both good and evil. We are capable of transforming the kindest animal into a vicious beast. Cruelty on the one hand and fear on the other, pervade our consciousness through our thinking. We can send evil in a glance. We can turn a useful plant into one most poisonous and pernicious. This thought of the ancient philosophers has penetrated religions. Clement of Alexandria was aware that people themselves belittle great Creation, and now people may observe how evil can transform the gentlest of beings.

Of course, any tamer of beasts will tell you that very often it is kindness that helps them in their craft. However, they also know that, aside from goodness, preventive measures should be taken, depending on the character of the animal. This science could be called *expediency*. We can refrain from condemning the World, and at the same ponder the question of how malice came to enter it. Likewise, preventive measures can emerge not from evil but from the good.

Every Leader would do well to recall the Commandment of the ancient philosophers.

142. We have spoken before about the apathy of certain individuals. What is to be done when they are to be found among the very best? Apathy has crept into the broadest circles. Even apparent champions of the good indulge in spiritual apathy, while those who represent the darkness so rarely suffer from the same flaw.

There is a fairy tale in which the devil meets an Angel: The light-bearing one says: "Your servants are bitter!" And the devil replies: "Mine may be bitter, but yours are sour; we both must seek the sweet." The Angel hangs his head and is quiet, unable to point out any that had not soured. Thus the tendency has long been recognized.

143. Any path of evil can be abandoned in favour of the good. However, such opportunities are most clearly evident in tasks involving progression. Indeed, any tarrying in evil carries one away from the good with progressive speed. So, while yesterday it was possible to jump off the chariot of evil, it is no longer possible to return to the same spot today. Let this be a reminder to anyone who thinks that the burden of evil may be

thrown off just as easily at any point. Evil is a sticky substance, overgrown with small truths, the like of which We have spoken before.

144. People who have taken upon themselves the Great Service can be called *Heavenly Stones*. In striving they become full and overflowing with Light; they pierce the lowest layers, while concealing a diamond within — an adamant. It is not easy to be a diamond; one must root oneself in the Light in order to overcome the darkness. Great Service knows no rest. Spirit is strengthened by keeping permanent vigilance. Many small earthly truths should be covered with a dome of magnanimity. One should take cover in the Light emanating from the Hierarchy. One should comprehend that the Subtle and Fiery Worlds are inherent in the very nature of things.

One may not notice the sun from inside a pit, yet people study stars from inside a well. The most unexpected things happen on the path of Service, but the experienced Leader will never forget that every worldly loss is compensated for in space.

145. Nowhere do people think about Living Ethics. They think that it is possible to live through ordinary measures, but with each passing day it becomes clearer that people can best be saved through a faith that is above all religions. There is not much of such faith; and let us not attempt to count in the thousands something that would be sufficient when counted by the dozen. Extraordinary are the paths of becoming conscious of the Supreme.

146. The word *choir* is understood to denote a consonance of voices, yet there can also be a choir of energies, a choir of hearts, a choir of fires. In teaching attention should be paid to the principle of the choir, which in no way encroaches on the principle of the individual. Cultivating cooperation in this way brings about a direct increase in potential. Thought for the choral principle unites with creation. People can understand that a chorus must consist of a variety of participants. Only highly experienced leaders understand how necessary participants are who, although they may not be the most active, bring an originality to the harmony. The Teacher rejoices at every new manifestation of originality, for it is here that a new kind of fire is born.

147. Let us look at how nations feel the significance of knowledge. We shall take care to ensure that the manifestation of knowledge takes an unusual path, one that will ignite the imagination. Indeed, it is not easy to awaken the imagination of past incarnations. Only a purified consciousness that is no longer disconcerted by the prospect of spiritual transition is capable of being continually, tirelessly, and uniquely imaginative.

148. The basic law must be assimilated that the Teacher gives direction, but does not insist on the details. Each must seek and find through their own efforts. People have but a vague understanding of the greatness of the law that directs us to make new discoveries for ourselves. Not only now, but even in better years people have demanded ready-made formulas, instead of ones they have thought out themselves. How instructive are tests in which the disciple must find an entire word on the basis of the first letter! But few will seek such a unified consciousness. It might also be pointed out how much this kind of searching strengthens leadership.

149. On many occasions philosophers have noted that gathering people together is permissible only when it leads to moral results. Indeed, this truth is new to our time. When people gather together the consequences are often a distortion of the most basic foundations. Let us look at the subtle and fiery environment of such large gatherings. Let us look and be terrified: for discordant rhythms admit only the lowest entities and transform fiery messages into a scorching fire. If it is difficult for a virtuous visitor to make their way through a bestial crowd, then more subtle beings will be cast away, like dry leaves by a whirlwind. Must We await the time when advice on the impact of the masses will be given during classes on psychology? People are willing to accept governance, yet are reluctant to cultivate their own will.

150. The Leader does not allow himself to become upset over seeming failures, for he knows that there is more than enough good in the world to fill any abyss. He will sense every deviation from the path, yet each deviation will simply provide him with another opportunity to visit a new region. Similarly, in the hands of the Leader the good becomes a true manifestation of Light. Consolation lies not in the impossibility of failure, but in knowing that every achievement of the good is the manifestation of a new success. I do not advise you to count signs of darkness, for they will only lead you into the gloom. There is but one Light, and the Light may act as a yardstick and a source of support. The Fiery World was created by the Light, and thought is a product of Fire.

151. People usually fail to notice even pivotal circumstances. Yesterday I directed your attention to people's reluctance to understand what they themselves are doing! The ladder was built long ago, but people still rush headlong into emptiness, because they are thinking about a previous ladder. It is impossible to concentrate people's thoughts on reality. The simplest and most beautiful solutions are passed over in silence and negated just because their grandfather's ladder once stood somewhere else. It disappeared long ago, yet the limited consciousness will not accept this reality. May the magnificence of the Fiery World at least advance people's steps towards the rungs of reality!

152. One should observe how entire countries can become shaken by a single misconception. One cannot excuse this simply by saying that someone was unaware of something. Usually proof can be found that such knowledge was knocking at all the doors; was lying on all the desks and was referred to many times. It is not fair to excuse inattention or unwillingness to delve into thought. New oppressions amount to nothing more than doubtful behaviour on the part of the Leader. Often the people cannot see the actual cause, yet they feel in their hearts that it is doubtful. Most of all, the Leader must guard herself against a growing lack of credibility.

153. Forfeiture of blessing is an act characteristic of the most ancient Patriarchate. It is far removed from the later anathema. An anathema is a product of ignorance, but the more ancient act implied rupturing all connection with the Hierarchy. Connection with the Hierarchy constitutes a true blessing with all its consequences.

The ignorant will contest: "We have many times defamed the Supreme, and nevertheless we still exist — no fire has burnt us, and nothing threatens us!" Then let us lead them to the square where blind beggars are crawling in the filth, and tell them: "Look, here you are!" Let us lead them into prisons, let us lead them into mines, let us lead them to conflagrations, let us lead them to places of execution, and tell them: "Do you not recognize yourselves? Once you cut the thread with the Supreme, you fall headlong into the abyss." There is no need to frighten anyone, for life is filled with such horrors as it is. Remember that while the tension of fire is invisible, nothing is immune to its consequences. So you can see how even the ancients understood the law of justice and how they were aware even then that the consequences of abusing the Principles are so grave and terrible that they cannot be immediate.

154. The Leader should not overshadow historical events with any personal feeling. It is unacceptable to tinge the events of a whole people with personal joy or sorrow. Many events have been distorted by personal arbitrariness, which has infected broad aspirations with violence. The Leader must manifest high levels of cooperation in order to safeguard the people's creative enthusiasm. Rarely has cooperation such as a merger of cosmic forces succeeded in becoming established. Of course, only the transfer of consciousness into the future can protect the Leader from her personal sense of the past.

155. Do not be surprised that We fill space with a name when We wish to notify you of something. We confirm Our decision in space. Those who understand the connection to the Hierarchy should also grasp that the decision of the World depends on what is filling space. After all, it is not the earthly world that decides, but the whole triad of Worlds. Thus, even the seemingly most agreed-upon earthly resolutions are destroyed, if they have not been accepted by the two Higher Worlds. Also the dark forces must be notified sometimes, because their howl only goes to intensify the noise of any announcement. Such a call spreads throughout all the worlds and awakens new energies. Of course, those whom such a manifestation concerns must be careful, for the whirlwind is moving in their direction.

156. The main danger lies in the incredible divergence of consciousness. While some are almost touching upon atomic energy, others have not yet reached that of the caveman. This discrepancy gives rise to a confusion of currents and hampers movement. It is easier to move troglodytes than such diverse crowds. This is why the advancement and the expansion of consciousness have become so complicated.

157. New methods should be applied in everything. You can see how world events are being forged by new swords. Study international law to avoid falling into old methods. You see how events are unfolding in Germany, Italy, Turkey; there is no provision for events such as these in international law. It could be said that the path of the world has extended beyond the old law. We are not looking for rights, but for justice.

158. Think of both your country and your family in terms of self-sufficiency. Picture how a people can exist via internal exchange, how a family can think in spiritual terms; in this way a people can assert themselves and come to love advancement.

159. Yes, yes, yes, if people do not turn to the Hierarchy for inspiration, then much perturbation will occur. Balance and concordance have been disturbed by a mechanical worldview. Half a century ago, We were concerned for the multiplication of physical knowledge. Indeed, much has been achieved in this area, yet at the same time spiritual consciousness has lagged behind the physical. Ethics have been lost amidst piles of formulas. Machines have distracted human beings from the art of thinking. There are enough robots now! The heart is needed for the balance of the world; in this Edict is your urgent salvation to be found. A dark will is pressing upon Earth's aura.

160. An experienced landowner will find a use for waste of any kind. This heroic deed must be assumed by every contemporary Builder. It is a particularly onerous task, for it is not easy to make use of robots when conscious substantiation is required.

161. Let us strive to understand what is most essential. The ability to determine degrees of necessity is a quality of leadership. One must be able to arrange numerous simultaneous requests into a mosaic of general and consecutive order. Neither logic nor reason, nor formula, but the fire of the heart will illumine the path of successive action. One must be able to comprehend with one's whole heart where there is sufficient space for passage, so as not to jostle one's neighbour. The heart will indicate when one should avoid applying pressure. Such tests of strength are known as the wings of justice.

162. Shame on the country where teachers dwell in poverty and misery! Shame on those who are aware that their children are taught by those suffering hardship! There is not only disgrace in a people that fails to take care of the teachers of its future generation, it is also a sign of its ignorance. Can a nation's children really be entrusted to the despondent? Can one really forget the emanation of sorrow? Can one really fail to know how incapable a depressed spirit is of evoking rapture? Can one really consider teaching a worthless profession? Can one really expect children to become spiritually enlightened if the school is a place of humiliation and insult? Can one really sense new creation against a background of gnashing teeth? Can one really expect to feel the fires of the heart when the spirit is silent? Let us say, let us repeat, that in forgetting its teachers, a people forgets its future. Let us not waste a single hour and direct our thoughts towards the joys of the future! Let us recognize that the teacher should be the most valued face of a country's establishments. The time is approaching when the spirit must be educated and gladdened by true knowledge. The Fire is at the threshold.

163. The hearts of teachers should be softened in order for them to maintain a constant state of learning. The hearts of children know what burns and what has been extinguished. Striving together with the teacher, rather than studying assigned lessons, will make for a marvellous world. Opening the eyes of pupils means coming to love the great creation with them. Who would disagree that to aim one's arrow far, one must be standing on solid ground? Any archer will confirm this. So let us learn to take good care of everything that affirms the future. The Fire is at the threshold.

164. There is a reason that the ancient sages advised taking up arts and crafts. Everyone had to be familiar with this kind of manual work. It served as a means of concentration. In striving towards perfection, each paid special attention to their will and awareness. Even in those few objects that have been preserved, one sees sophisticated levels of craftsmanship.

And now the time has come to return to the quality of manual work. Spiritual limitation must not be determined by machines. One must devote one's time to the quality of manual work; this will revive powers of imagination. Quality and imagination are united on the rungs of fiery achievement. May the Leader remember the advice of the ancient sages.

Indeed, it is important to understand the sources of antiquity. When their significance is revealed, new discoveries will be made. Much may be found, but these treasures must not become subject to primitive intention. Let us not detract from the right-mindedness of evolution.

165. The spite of nonbelief is flooding the world. This is the fiercest form of malice, for it competes with the very essence of Existence. It irritates itself and in its falsehood destroys all potential.

166. Often people ask, "What about the wills of the departed?" Frequently their instructions are not in line with the opinions

of those who execute them. Except for fratricidal proposals, one may suggest that all the rest be fulfilled. One should refrain from adopting the karma of others, not least because the departed continue to develop energy in the direction they took in life. After all, it is very difficult to change a conviction that is still held in the Subtle World. Therefore, the execution of last wills is very beneficial to the harmony of energies.

167. Often the Leader loses charm on account of a most insignificant habit. Also, the Leader's halo may grow dim from an inability to restrain his emotions. The Leader must set an example of balance, for it is only by these means that he can demonstrate the great reserve of his psychic energy. As soon as the Leader permits himself a habit or becomes immersed in the mundane and material, he will become ordinary. Every mundane trait is a grave for one's heroic feats.

168. And so, no matter where you stand, there are always three paths ahead: the easy one, the difficult one, and the terrible one. The first path is paved by a comprehension of all successful, useful, and noble combinations. The second is when a number of good combinations are covered by intensely harmful, destructive constructions. This is a difficult path and to take it is like running with your eyes blindfolded. The third path is when you are pulled by ignorance into the darkness of decomposition — this path is terrible indeed. People have no right to blame others for this horror, for they themselves have closed their eyes and ears. They have rejected help and allowed chaos to enter their thinking. May the Builder follow the first path.

169. Can the Light enter into an alliance with the darkness? The Light would have to extinguish itself in order to unite with its opposite element. A Leader of the Light should not even consider accepting into her camp extinguishers and opponents of the Light. The Light cannot increase the darkness, just as the darkness cannot increase the Light — such unions are a contradiction of Nature.

170. The right path is good in that each of its dimensions is inherently of some benefit. It is futile even to ponder the limits of such a path. There is no limit to the extent to which one can improve.

171. A diver prepares himself for the deepest layers of water. He is not concerned about the upper layer, but he does need to account for the pressure he will encounter in the deepest layer. In the same way, when interacting with a nation's people, the Leader must have some idea of the lowest level of consciousness. Understanding the lowest level of consciousness should never be neglected. On the contrary, the Leader must equip herself with such resourcefulness that she may discern a human sound within a bestial roar.

Thus, one must have ready a large reserve of different explanations in order to speak with those of each layer in accordance with their consciousness. The inability to adapt to the consciousness of another is a dangerous thing. Much misfortune has resulted from a single word uttered out of place! Demonstrate resourcefulness!

172. A messenger overtaken by pursuers drives his horse into the widest stretch of the river. The pursuers stop, hoping that the messenger will drown, but he makes it to the far shore. To speed their chase, the pursuers hasten to the narrowest stretch they can find, but here they drown in the current. Truly, the narrow stretch is dangerous — this consideration should be applied to everything. Seeking the mirage of ease will not lead to heroic feats. What is most difficult is what is most accessible.

People are unwilling to understand that persistent searching awakens powerful energies. Therefore, let us not rush to the narrow stretch but rather seek the broad.

173. It has been said that humanity must abandon luxury. Not without reason have people paid particular attention to this concept. Nothing can replace luxury. It is neither beauty, nor spirituality, nor improvement, nor creation, nor compassion, nor kindness — no good concept can replace it. Luxury represents the destruction of resources and opportunities. Luxury represents decay, for any construction beyond the divine rhythm can only represent decay. One can see clearly enough that mundane luxury has already been shaken, yet one should still seek concordant cooperation in order to cure the infection of luxury.

Selfishness will object that luxury is an earned abundance. People will also say that luxury is regal — but this would be slander. Luxury has always been a sign of decline and darkening of the spirit. The chains of luxury are just as terrible for the Subtle World, where what is required is advancement and constant improvement of thought. Any encumbrance will block the path to the next Gate.

174. Do not make fixed plans. There are many new conditions in space. One may cling to solid walls, and the plan must be solid in its foundations, but the details must be allowed to develop along with world events.

175. First and foremost the wise Leader listens to his interlocutor, and only then voices his opinion. He listens not only to understand the essence of the thought expressed, but also to understand the language of his interlocutor. The latter condition is far from insignificant. There is no great victory when legislators are the only ones who can understand their laws.

The fundamentals of Existence must resonate with all and to each according to their own understanding.

Thus, the art of comprehending the language of one's interlocutor is related to the great development of consciousness. This is mastered by inspiration received from the Hierarchy or by the conscious refinement of attention. There is no arrogance in this — on the contrary, it reflects great sympathy for the concept of *interlocutor*. Many useful insights are undermined by peculiarity of expression, yet a fiery eye will discern those grains of truth.

176. Any suggestion of impossibility stems from the dark essence. It is important to eradicate all despondency, for this is not a path that leads to the Truth. People of the most diverse nationalities express joy and sorrow in the same way. Hence the path to mutual understanding is open.

177. It is unacceptable, even indirectly, to violate the foundations of cooperation. The concept of *cooperation* should be associated with the concepts of teachership, as well as respect for your neighbour, yourself, and those who follow after you. Especially at the current time, one must not diminish the significance of cooperation as a means of expanding consciousness. One must come to love cooperation as a guarantee of common prosperity.

178. People are unable to think about the future, for they are all too often held under the spell of past illusions. Let us imagine a person who many days later receives bad news about something which happened long ago. The event no longer exists, and the person himself has lived for a long time since the incident, yet he immerses himself in the past and loses connection with the future. After all, the tree of the future must grow, and one cannot fell it through immersion in the past. Schools should pay attention to studying the future. Each Leader in their field will think about the future; they who do not, cannot be called Leaders.

179. It has already been said that blasphemy must be cast aside; it is important to understand that each and every case of blasphemy is unacceptable. Sometimes people eradicate blasphemy within a narrow circle of ideas, and yet their tongues still gravely blaspheme their neighbours. Who can judge what exalted wires of the heart may be affected by this evil defamation? Hence blasphemy must be altogether expelled from life as a reproachful, harmful action.

180. The ignorant believe that the Radiant One will come to avenge the darkness. However, the Light does not in fact annihilate the darkness. Rather, what happens is that the darkness is crushed and destroyed when it approaches the Light. It is essential to understand that the darkness annihilates itself when it nears the Light.

The Leader should remember this when the ignorant speak of revenge.

181. After a state council meeting, a certain ruler took an earthenware vase and smashed it in front of everyone. When he was asked about the meaning of what he had done, he replied: "I'm simply reminding you that some things are irreparable." When we break the simplest object, we understand that it is irreparable, and yet how irreparable are the actions of our thoughts! We are accustomed to surrounding ourselves with crude notions, which in turn have ousted all supreme ideas. If rulers reminded us more often of the irreparability of our decisions in thought, they would prevent much misfortune.

A ruler is a living example. A ruler is a paver of paths across all worlds. She lays the grounds for prosperity — and not only on the physical plane. Thus, those for whom Fire exists only at the end of a match can never be rulers. Her magnitude will be equal to her ideas.

182. Whoever says that there is no need for heroes cuts themselves off from evolution. Note that mediocrity, unbelief, and selfishness, are invariably accompanied by self-destruction. It may take decades for this process of self-devouring to be detected, but it will begin the moment that the Hierarchy is first denied.

It is impossible to imagine progressive movement without the Hierarchy. One must constantly repeat this simple Teaching, for many people are heading towards the abyss. Rays from the energy centres of the shoulders cause tortuous pain — caused not by planetary convulsions, but by humanity's own rasping. As tornadoes separate water into columns, so humanity now divided has started to spin. This is a highly significant year for the uprising of the human spirit. Fire can be held back only to a certain extent. It will inevitably break through everything that obstructs its path.

183. Every desecration of the Saviour, the Teacher, and Heroes plunges the people into savagery and submerges them in chaos. How is one to explain that chaos is all too near, that it does not have to cross an ocean before it reaches you? It is equally as difficult to make people understand that savagery begins with the very small. When the treasure of solemnity has been lost and the pearls of the knowledge of the heart have been scattered, what is left?!

One may remember how people scoffed at the Great Sacrifice. Has not the whole world incurred responsibility for this savagery? One can see it reflected in moral degeneration. Degeneration is worst of all! I say: May all energies be blessed, but by all accounts, avoid lapsing into the insanity of decay. Let us remember all the Great Days!

184. One can imagine how beautiful the common service of multitudes of people must be when their hearts are brought together in unified ascent. Let us not say "It is impossible" or "It is rejected." One can draw upon the Divine Power and become illumined by the Light — but one must know wherein Divine Light and Power lie. Some may laugh, but they laugh in the darkness. What could be more awful than laughter emerging from the darkness! Yet the Light will be with those who thirst for it.

185. Cooperation based on personal feelings is fragile. Besides respect for labour itself, reverence of the Hierarchy is essential. Under a whirlwind of personal feelings people, like cork manikins, rush to and fro, jostle and spasmodically connect. But by its very nature, no work will tolerate spasmodic activity. Labour is a fiery action, and yet the fire must never be allowed to become fitful. In addition, external personal feelings can interfere with the discerning of new opportunities. Many beautiful actions have suffered from a transitory personal mirage!

186. Technocracy should be regarded as a trick of the servants of darkness. Dark forces have turned many times to technical solutions. Their hope is to occupy human attention, only to distract it from spiritual growth. However, the problem of life can be solved solely through the expansion of consciousness. Observe how easily mechanical hypotheses capture people's hopes. For the ancients it was Maya, which could be broken by the slightest nudge.

187. But it is clear that people want their existence to change. One ruler, for example, wanted to find a contented person. After a long search, the ruler found one — the person was deaf, dumb, and blind.

188. The path of joyful heroic deeds is a hundred times shorter than the path of dismal duties. How firmly the pilgrims of the fiery march must remember this commandment! Only the sign of a heroic feat will lift them above danger, but the significance of the heroic feat must be cultivated within the heart as the joy of the spirit. One may fail to notice the best path if one's eyes do not follow the star of the heroic feat. Even the darkest corners must be illumined with the one Light. No thing, and no one, will ever force us to turn back into the darkness!

189. Reverie must be transformed into disciplined thinking. The ancient sages advised mothers to tell their children epic tales and acquaint them with the best songs of heroic deeds. Will humanity really now renounce these wise precepts?

Above all the Fiery World is open to heroes and selfless devotees.

190. The gaze of the Leader is directed towards the future.

191. When will humanity finally learn wherein lies the true dignity of a people? When will humanity finally realize that the innermost spirit must be protected and that the bearers of thought can properly guide a nation, as a single source? Similarly, the annihilation of thought can deprive a people of its power or confirmed influence. Therefore, more than anything else, a people must take care of their Helmsperson, for a boat without a helm cannot save them in a storm. For this reason the great care of the people and every organizing process must

be based on the Hierarchy, for every structure must be imbued with Power from Above.

Thus, until an understanding of the Hierarchy is affirmed, humanity will sink into the ignorance and gloom of decay.

192. What state can flourish without a great Leader? What established undertaking can exist without a Lord? One must truly understand that the concept of *Leader* represents the synthesis of one's highest aspirations. Hence only the concept of the Hierarchy of the Light-bearing Leader can give direction to spirit.

So let everyone, one and all, consider well and remember the Power of the Hierarchy. Only through this understanding is it possible to advance. Only through this understanding is it possible to achieve. Let everyone remember that each stone thrown against the Hierarchy will turn into a mountain against themselves. So let everyone remember. This is how We proclaim the Leader-Hierarch.

193. Every spirit creates its own karma. Every people forms its own karma. Of course, nations are seeking a Leader, for even established prestige is insufficient to keep from falling those who think falsely. Neither gold, nor flashy names, nor reams of worthless advice can save a nation. True fiery thought, and the fiery spirit of the Leader, will open up new paths. Therefore, during this time of cosmic perturbation, let the star of the Spiritual Leader shine brightly!

Thus, on the ruins of the Old World, let the Great Realm of Light rise!

∽

GLOSSARY

ALTAI SISTERS — the idea of a Women's Union, also known as the Sisters of the Golden Mountain.

Helena Roerich described this union in the following manner: "The idea of a Community of Heroic Sisters has been my dream since childhood. I imagined these heroines bringing light and joy to the most remote corners and into the hardest conditions of life anywhere in our motherland. Of course, as my consciousness expanded, so did the dreams. Hence, all fields of life should be reflected in such a Community; some Sisters devote themselves to healing, others to agriculture, still others could be teachers or talented lecturers in various branches of knowledge as well as social planning, able to expound ideas in plain language accessible to the masses. Of course, the study of arts and crafts and their teaching would have a prominent place in this Community. And the introduction of the principles of *Living Ethics* would adorn and crown all the heroines' noble activities.

"The cells of the Community would be widely scattered, and the Sisters should gather in small groups and travel to inspect and observe in the districts assigned to them. It would take a whole army of such female workers to meet all the needs of the masses as well as to satisfy their spiritual and physical hunger. Schools should be established near the Central Community, as well as universities, laboratories, an institute for research in psychic energy, and all sorts of workshops, sanatoria, cooperatives, model farms, etc. — in short, a whole city of knowledge could be built. Speaking of these Heroic Sisters, the Great Teacher put it so beautifully: Let them become dear to people. Let people say, 'A dear one came to our village.' My Heroic Sisters should first of all manage to become dear to the people."[1]

---

[1] Helena Roerich, *Pis'ma* [Letters], vol. 3 (Moscow: Mezhdunarodnyy tsentr Rerikhov, 2001), p. 241.

ARMAGEDDON — the Final Battle between the Forces of Light and darkness, as proclaimed in ancient prophecies. If the Powers of Light are headed by the Great Lord of Shambhala, then the forces of evil are led by the Lord of Darkness, also known as Lucifer (*Latin*, "Light-Bearer").

The ancient legend of the Fallen Angel, who rebelled against the Powers of Light and became Satan, reflects a true drama that took place on Earth millions of years ago.

Lucifer was one of the Eight Great Spirits, who, in an act of self-sacrifice, left their worlds nearly eighteen million years ago and came to Earth in order to assist and edify humanity. Lucifer had quickly ascended the Ladder of Evolution and achieved many triumphs in his World. Of all the Teachers, his Spirit was energetically closest to Earth, as well as having all the features of the composition of Saturn. This gave him the right to participate in the development of humanity, particularly its intellect. Like the other Great Teachers who had been incarnated and were interacting with humankind, he endowed them with reason and free will.

During the times of Atlantis, while living among people, the Great Teachers imparted to them an abundance of secret knowledge, enabling them to achieve success in many spheres of life — they were able to manage the most powerful energies; they knew the mysteries of Nature and could breed new species of plants and animals; they could create the most complex technologies, including the science of aeronautics; in addition, they made direct contact with Distant Worlds.

Being an expert on all the mysteries of Earth, Lucifer justifiably become known as the Prince of this World. It also left him with a special attachment to Earth, while the remaining Seven Great Teachers were subject to the attraction of the Higher Worlds and managed to preserve their purity. With every new incarnation on this planet, Lucifer's higher consciousness gradually darkened. Pride totally captured his mind which led to his downfall and revolt against the Laws of the Cosmos.

Having lost the right to bear this name, Lucifer thought to limit the whole of humanity solely to Earth, depriving it of a connection to Higher and Distant Worlds. Demonstrating the miracles of matter, he rapidly gained adherents, and these soon constituted the majority of the population of Atlantis. Lack of heart development among humans meant that they were vulnerable to temptation.

To achieve his goal of becoming the absolute and only god for Earth-dwellers, Lucifer directed all his efforts towards demeaning Woman, which always and inevitably leads to the desensitization and degeneration of humanity. He destroyed the Cult of Spirit, creating instead a cult of personality: the Atlanteans began to build temples and monuments to themselves. People began to use secret knowledge not for the good of all but for the accumulation of wealth, inventing deadly weapons, waging war, practising dark magic, and so on. Those who warned of the inevitable disaster resulting from the actions of the Atlanteans faced penalty of death.

In this way, the violation of Cosmic Laws on such an unprecedented scale, along with the use of dark magic by the Atlanteans against the Sons of Light, brought destructive elemental forces into play. These gradually destroyed Atlantis and ushered in the Ice Age, in which entire regions of the planet were covered with ice.

Many peoples of the world have preserved legends of the Battle of the Titans, or the Battle of the Gods, that tell of the time when a group of Gods opposed another dominant God. These myths actually reflect events connected with the rebellion of the Sons of Light, the Titans of Shambhala, against the dictatorship of Lucifer and his evil sorcerers, which took place during the later days of Atlantis. In 9564 BCE the Light secured a victory over the warlocks of Poseidonis, the last island of Atlantis, as it sank beneath the waves.

Prior to these disasters, the Sons of Light resettled in Egypt the finest and most spiritual inhabitants of Atlantis, thereby transferring the entire Atlantean sacred heritage. The Masters themselves moved to Shambhala, at that time also an island, and have been assisting humanity secretly ever since, never revealing their identity.

At the onset of a new stage in human development, the Fallen Angel founded and headed the dark brotherhood, becoming a furious enemy of the Great Brotherhood of Teachers for all ages to come. In contrast to Shambhala, located high in the mountains, the dark brotherhood established its stronghold at the lowest point, burrowing into subterranean layers closer to Earth's core, in order to gain strength from its fire. But at this point, Lucifer decided to convince humanity that he did not exist, in order to more easily deceive and enslave. One should never underestimate the hierophants of evil, because they know many secrets of Nature and the human mind. Their main goal was to sever humanity's connection with the Great Teachers, so that even the smallest reminder of the Brotherhood would be persecuted vigorously by humanity itself.

Nevertheless, in the not too distant past the Messengers of Light succeeded in turning the situation around. At this point the forces of darkness realized that they would never triumph over the Light and, sooner or later, would be annihilated by fiery energies approaching Earth. Therefore, Lucifer, who had no access to the Higher Worlds, decided to blow up the planet, since this alone would enable him to remain in its atmosphere for some time ahead, thereby prolonging his life. The catastrophe could have taken place in 1899, 1949, 1954, 1977, or 1999. Had it occurred, the Brotherhood of Great Teachers, together with the most spiritually advanced Earth-dwellers, would have moved in subtle body form to Venus and Jupiter; the souls of the majority would have waited billions of years for the formation of a new planet on which to continue humanity's evolution. The evil ones would have ended up on Saturn. All planets and stars in the Universe are home to living beings, it is just that in each case the structure of matter has different degrees of tenuity. Therefore, people cannot see them either with the naked eye or with telescopic devices, which are as yet far from perfect. Nevertheless, the Earth was saved from destruction through the combined incredible efforts of all Forces of Light in the Solar System.

The liberation of Earth from Lucifer's dictatorship began on the Subtle Plane at the end of the 19th century and the turn of the 20th century; soon afterwards the battle shifted onto the physical plane in the form of the First World War, 1914–1918. At the end of 1931, a new phase in the struggle for humanity's freedom and immortality began on the Subtle Plane. The calculations unearthed in the Great Pyramid of Giza indicated the significance of 1936 — this date marked the start of a personal fight between the Great Lord of Shambhala and the Lord of Darkness, the celestial battle of Archangel Michael and his angels with the Dragon, as proclaimed in the Bible. Eventually, the decisive battle between the Forces of Light and the darkness shifted from the Subtle Plane to the physical plane giving rise to the Second World War, 1939–1945.

The second phase of the Final Battle ended with the triumph of the Forces of Light on 17 October 1949, when the Great Lord banished Lucifer to Saturn.

However, after their defeat, the hierophants of evil managed to gather the remainder of their crushed army on the Subtle Plane. Their desire for revenge resulted in the third phase of the Final Battle which began at the end of the 20th century. This stage of the battle was reflected on the earthly plane in Chechnya, Nagorno-Karabakh, the Caucasus, Transnistria, the former republics of Yugoslavia, and then in Syria and Ukraine, where some of the Points of Life most significant to the current time are located. But, in general, from time immemorial, in places where Points of Life were born, involutionary forces of evil have tried to establish power by means of local or global bloody war, spawning their own Points of Death.

Nevertheless, the main field of the Final Battle lies in each human heart. It will come to an end towards the final days of 21st century, when the last bearer of darkness on Earth and in the near-Earth spheres will be expelled to Saturn in the wake of their ruler.

Lucifer's rebellion against Cosmic Laws greatly slowed the evolution of Earth. If it were not for Lucifer, there would be no borders today between the physical world and the Higher Spheres, and humanity would be unfamiliar with the phenomenon of death. Furthermore, in attempting to separate the Earth from the Distant Worlds, the forces of darkness obscured the Subtle Plane of the atmosphere around the planet so that energies from the Sun and other stars, sent to assist humanity, could not penetrate. This same process contributed to parts of the planet being covered with ice. Its melting in the present age is a sign of the Fiery Era, in which there is no place for cold in any manifestation. This means that Earth is gradually being released from the "heritage" of Atlantis and that its atmosphere is being purified. However, for centuries having been deprived of new stellar energies, people are unaccustomed to them. Hence it is only the willingness and desire on the part of humanity to assimilate these new energies that can bring about the complete destruction of the heavy dirty-grey atmosphere, which is suffocating the entire planet, as it is seen from the Subtle Plane.

AURA — the electro-magnetic radiation of all the accumulated energies of a living organism, especially the heart, retaining its dominant colour, sound, and scent. All bodies and objects of the manifest world are surrounded by an aura.

The human aura is a kind of passport which quickly identifies the individual's essence and destiny. In the future, a person's aura will determine their suitability to hold important positions in every domain of life. Every thought, emotion, feeling, or act leaves an imprint on the aura in the form of radiations, which, in turn, magnetically attract elements from space that correspond with their tonality. The more powerful the fiery energy in a person, the stronger the influence of their aura over their whole environment. Throughout their lives, people suffuse everything they touch with the radiations of their aura, brightening or darkening the objects around them. In addition every individual perceives the world through the prism of their aura, as though they were looking through a pair of glasses. Hence, through a light aura, one perceives only the Light, and through a dark aura, one perceives the darkness.

The aura of a newborn child is colourless until the first gleam of consciousness imbues it with colours that correspond to the accumulations of previous lives. As a rule, this happens at the age of seven.

The auric field should be enclosed by a protective net, woven together from the sediment of the subtlest fiery energies providing a shield against extraneous intrusions and influences. But souls devoid of spirituality lack this protection causing them often to fall victim to the impact of other people's auras, especially those that possess a powerful aura of dark fire; they also succumb to the influence of various evil entities from the Subtle Plane. First and foremost this affects a person's health. Remember that more spiritually-minded people have a protective net in the form of fiery ruby sparks. However, dark entities are always attempting to break through, for even the slightest rupture opens the way to gaining control over another being. The aura of powerful spirits generates a ray, which imbues thoughts — or anything else — with its colour and energy. When a thought like this is aimed in a specific direction, it has the appearance of a real ray in space and is equipped with tremendous power.

A planet possesses an aura, too, along with a protective net. The aura of Earth accumulates all the energies produced by the activity and free will of humanity. At the beginning of its existence, the aura of the Earth was golden, but by the mid-20th century it had turned ash-grey with clouds of brown gas and black holes in its protective net. By the end of the last century, the Hierarchy of Light and its earthly colleagues managed to restore the net. However, the state of the planet's aura still depends upon humanity and upon each and every individual.

AVATARS (*Sanskrit*, "descent") — Gods, Spirits of the Higher Spheres and Distant Worlds incarnated in the bodies of ordinary mortals. Referred to in Tibet by the ancient word *Lha* (*Tibetan*, "Spirit," "God"), whose meaning covers the entire series of celestial Hierarchies. Every Supreme Cosmic Concept is personified in a High Spirit that also takes a human form. For this reason every ancient religion has a pantheon of Gods, each embodying a certain Idea and representing a particular Force of Nature.

Sons of God, Sons of Light, Sons of Heaven, Sons of Fire, Sons of Reason, Archangels, Planet Regents, Masters of Wisdom, Bodhisattvas (*Sanskrit*, "Enlightenment Beings"), the Dhyan Chohans (*Sanskrit*, "Lords of Light"), the Rishis (*Sanskrit*, "Sages of Insight"), the Kumaras (*Sanskrit*, "Youths"), and so on — all High Spirits, who, like the Avatars, assumed a human appearance to raise the consciousness of humanity and accelerate its development. Seven Great Spirits took on the role of caring for planet Earth and humanity. Again and again, they were incarnated as the greatest founders of kingdoms, religions, sciences, and philosophies to help people realize their divine nature. As such, they have left deep traces in every area of life and in every land.

For example, their incarnations on Earth include Akbar the Great, Anaxagoras, Apollonius of Tyana, Confucius, the Count of Saint-Germain, Francis of Assisi, Gautama Buddha, Giordano Bruno, Hermes Trismegistus, Jakob Böhme, Jesus Christ, John the Apostle, Joseph, Joshua, King Arthur, Krishna, Lao-Tzu, Mahatma Koot Hoomi, Mahatma Morya, Melchizedek, Menes, Moses, Muhammad, Numa Pompilius, Origen, Orpheus, Paul the Apostle, Pericles, Plato, Pythagoras, Rama, Ramesses the Great, Sergius of Radonezh, Solomon, Thomas à Kempis, Thutmose III, Tsongkhapa, Tutankhamun, Zoroaster, and many others.

All the Gods have a Spouse, with whom they are united in the Higher Worlds; one does not exist without the other. But, since the Masculine Principle must express itself in the visible aspect of life, and the Feminine Principle in the invisible aspect, Female Deities were revered as the most sacred and secret in all ancient religions. It is the Female Deities, incarnated on Earth as mothers, sisters, daughters, and wives who inspired the Sons of Light and the peoples of the Earth, as well as humanity as a whole through their self-sacrifice, heroism, and continuous giving. Similarly, the entire Hierarchy of Light devoutly honours the Mother of the World — the Great Spirit of the Feminine Principle, who is personified in many world religions as the Supreme Goddess. The Mother of the World incarnated as Mary to give life to Jesus Christ. Subsequently, for the past two thousand years, She has manifested through Her Hypostasis-Daughters — Faith, Hope, and Love, who have continuously replaced each other, at no point abandoning this world.

BROTHERHOOD — Community of the Seven Messengers of the Distant Worlds and their disciples, who have lived side by side with humanity on Earth for millions of years, developing the human mind and heart. The Brotherhood is usually referred to as *White* to indicate the White Light that, upon splitting, yields the seven colours of the rainbow, each of which symbolizes one of the Great Teachers, and vice versa — the seven colours of the rainbow that result in the White Light after fusion.

The previous Solar System was tasked with giving people knowledge and developing their intelligence. The present System aims to bring people closer to Love, and the focus of Love is the heart. Therefore, the Great Lords have divided themselves into two Lodges — Western and Eastern.

The Western Lodge — also known as the Brotherhood of Luxor or the Thebes Sanctuary, located in Egypt — was to provide knowledge, as well as to develop and expand human consciousness, with an emphasis on the mental body, the mind, the human intellect, to help take a step towards the heart. All the knowledge accumulated in the past and present Solar Systems resides exclusively in Egypt.

The Eastern Lodge — Shambhala or the Himalayan Brotherhood — was to develop the intuition of the heart, always bearing Love and serving the highest energies. In other words, the West is the mind, and the East is the heart. Ancient traditions have it that the Masters left the West for the East. Many people, in fact, left the Sanctuary in Egypt to move to the East. This happens approximately once every two thousand years.

At the end of the 19th century, before the start of Armageddon, all the Secret Schools and Ashrams of the Western Brotherhood were closed and moved to the Himalayas. All the Great Teachers who had worked in the world — holding Initiations and imparting knowledge — were also summoned to the Stronghold of Light in the Himalayas. Humanity was abandoned for a hundred years, but knowledge was still passed on through their disciples. However, there was no longer any direct contact between the Masters and the vast majority.

The Theban Sanctuary is now reopening and once again beginning to serve Love. While previously it worked through the Ray of Knowledge, now these two Sanctuaries — Eastern and Western — are uniting, their Rays interpenetrating, and imparting a single Ray of Love-Wisdom. Similarly, all the Great Lords who saturated humanity with as much knowledge as possible are now beginning to act in service to Love. Thus a Great Synthesis is being born, and the two Greatest Schools are merging into one, affirming a single path for the world: ascent up the steps of Wisdom through illumination of the human heart.

Chenrezig (*Tibetan*) — the Tibetan name of Avalokiteshvara, the Divine Buddha of Compassion; Protector of Tibet.

Chintamani (*Sanskrit*, "magical jewel") — Gift of the constellation of Orion to the planet Earth; the mystical Stone manifest as the Treasure of the World, which is destined to bring happiness and prosperity to all living beings. Its actual place of origin is Sirius, because when this event occurred Sirius was part of Orion.

The Chintamani is preserved at the very heart of Shambhala and maintains a connection with the fire-breathing cores of maternal stars, thanks to which the planet Earth still retains the orbit of her own revolution.

A fragment of the Chintamani can "travel" around the world, if the Seven Great Teachers make a unanimous decision to put it into the hands of their Messenger, who is destined to carry out a specific historical mission. And then the fragment returns of its own accord and merges literally with the Treasure that remained always within the boundaries of Shambhala.

DEVADATTA (*Sanskrit*, "God-given") — the cousin and brother-in-law of Gautama Buddha who was among the first to enter the Buddhist community, and became its first schismatic. After several attempts to kill the Buddha, he led part of the community away by founding one of his own. He went to hell (Avichi) for his evil deeds.

GHOOM — one of the oldest Tibetan monasteries in Darjeeling, India, also known as Yiga Choeling and referred to as the Old Ghoom Monastery to distinguish it from a newer temple in the same area. Founded in 1850 by Sokpo Sherab Gyatso, a Mongolian scholar, astrologer, monk, and tutor to the Eighth Panchen Lama, it is famous for its large statue of Maitreya Buddha. Sokpo Sherab Gyatso was a disciple of the Master Morya, who often visited the Ghoom Monastery. The Master's meetings with Blavatsky and the Roerichs also took place there.

GOD — the Divine, Unchangeable, Invariable, and Infinite Principle; the eternally Unknowable Cause of All that exists; omnipresent, all-pervading, visible and invisible spiritual Nature, which exists everywhere, in which everything lives, moves, and has its being; the Absolute, including the potential of all things as well as all universal manifestations. Upon being made manifest, out of its Absolute Oneness, God becomes the Absolute of infinite differentiation and its consequences — relativity and polarities. God has no gender and cannot be imagined as a human being. In the Holy Scriptures, God is Fire, God is Love — the one primeval energy that conceives the worlds.

Where this notion does not refer to the above, in ancient Teachings it has always denoted the totality of the working and intelligent Forces of Nature. Thus, the world is ruled by the Creative Forces of the Cosmos, together constituting the limitless Hierarchy of Light, which in the Bible is represented as Jacob's Ladder.

However, the Great Unknown was, is, and always will be hidden from the eyes of those who live in the manifested world. The Primal Cause, the Absolute, has been and will be unknowable — forever and always.

The traditional Christian concept of *God* refers to the Planetary Spirit, or a *Demiurge* (*Greek*, "creator") — the Supreme Lord or Ruler of Earth, who has lived out His human evolution and reached an unparalleled level of spiritual development. Together with other High Spirits that constitute the Hierarchy of Light, He is now responsible for the creation, preservation, and transfiguration of Earth.

The Planetary Spirit is androgynous because there is no gender separation on the higher planes of Existence — hence, the pronoun *He* is used merely for lack of a more appropriate one. The Planetary Spirit can manifest in various Aspects and Hypostases, including male and female in the binary world since He bears within Himself both Principles.

As a rule, the governing Hierarchy of Light for young planets, such as Earth, consists of High Spirits that originated in Distant Worlds, where they long ago completed the stage of Evolution now being faced by Earth. When humanity on any given planet reaches spiritual maturity, the Lords of Light, who arrived there from other Worlds, leave and are replaced by the worthy High Spirits who have completed their evolution on this, their native young planet.

From ancient sacred texts, it is evident that the Planetary Spirit of Earth is the Lord of Sirius. Even the Quran states that Allah is the Lord of Sirius. However, it should be borne in mind that the God described in the Old Testament is not the same as the Supreme Lord of Earth whom Christ calls His Father in the New Testament.

Sometimes He who is denoted by the name *the One and Only*, forms simultaneously several of His own Hypostases, as well as Individualities (under different names), and one that possesses a higher energy component serves another (we might even say, Himself) as a Master, Teacher, and Protector — either in the physical world or in the Ethereal, depending on the single goal that is set before His "emanating forms."

Thus, one of the Hypostases of the Lord of Sirius manifested on Earth was Melchizedek (*Hebrew*, "king of righteousness") mentioned in the Bible as a Priest of the Most High. In esoteric philosophy, He is the King and Father of the planet Earth and the Priest of the Ineffable One, or the One whose Name is Silence, and carries the same Name.

According to the ancient legends of Judaism and early Christianity, Melchizedek establishes the right to a special and ideal dignity and extraordinary priesthood, germane to both royalty and high priests. Melchizedek is the prototype of the Messiah. He is the head of eternal angels, and He is "King of peace; without father, without mother, without descent, having neither beginning of days, nor end of life; but made like unto the Son of God; abideth a priest continually" (Heb. 7: 2-3). Jesus Christ was "called of God a high priest after the order of Melchizedek" (Heb. 5:10).

In the ancient Melchizedekian teaching, it was asserted that Melchizedek was the first and principal incarnation of the Supreme God, while Christ was only the image of Melchizedek. It was believed that Christ had descended upon a man, Jesus, at his baptism, and that Melchizedek was a Heavenly Power, higher than Christ. According to their teachings, Melchizedek did for Angels what Christ was to do for humankind.

The last incarnation of Melchizedek took place about 6,000 years ago as the first Zoroaster, or Zarathustra, the founder of Zoroastrianism and prophet. Zoroaster was given the Revelation of Ahura Mazda, or the Creator, in the form of the holy scripture of the Avesta in the language of Zend, which is very close to the language of Senzar.

According to linguistic studies, the name *Zoroaster* translates as "the golden shining star" or "Golden Sirius." In Zoroastrianism, Sirius is especially revered, being called *Tishtrya*, "whom Ahura Mazda has established as a lord and overseer above all stars, in the same way as he has established Zarathustra above men." Only thirteen Zarathustra incarnations have been revealed to humanity, and each carried a sacred scripture which over time was lost, requiring the manifestation of a new cycle of secret knowledge.

The image of Melchizedek bears the seal of High Mystery; the main pages of His incarnations may be revealed only to those who have ascended the first rungs of Initiation.

The Nativity Mystery of the Stellar Spirit of Sirius in the Glorious Body on the Higher Planes of Earth occurred for the first time on 19 July 2017. This is significant not only to Earth and the Solar System but to all the constellations headed and supervised by Sirius. This Mystery of Light will never be repeated in the present Grand Cycle of Evolution.

GREAT LORD OF SHAMBHALA — Solar Hierarch that stands at the head of the Solar System's Hierarchy of Light; the Creator, Preserver, and Transfigurer of the Solar System; the Teacher of Teachers, Lord of the World, Lord of Civilization, Lord of the White Flame, Holder of the Wheel of Law; Prime mover of humanity's evolution on Earth, and everything that exists in the Solar System.

It should also be borne in mind that the Solar Hierarch has a Father — the Stellar Hierarch, the Planetary Spirit and the Lord of Sirius, who on Earth is known as Sanat Kumara in the Puranas, as well as the "Ancient of Days" in the Bible. The Father can manifest Himself in the Son, and therefore the Son may bear the same Names.

Occupying a predominant position in the Solar System, the Solar Hierarch is also manifested in the role of the Heads of the Hierarchical structures on each of the individual planets of the Solar System under certain Names, which can be both known and unknown. Only one who ascends the rungs of Initiation can be endowed with more extensive knowledge of vital activity, as well as the Ray manifestations and Emanations of the Solar Hierarch.

Many times He has incarnated among Earth-dwellers under different Names, amid different peoples and races in various eras of the planet's history. But His essence has forever remained unchanged, and His goal is always the same: to uplift humanity to the next stage of spirit. Whatever earthly garments He donned they could not veil His Light, and those unable to withstand His mighty empyreal fires reacted furiously with persecutions, torture, and killings. The long-suffering Lord, the "Great Sacrifice," bore the burden of Earth on His shoulders.

The Solar Hierarch is the Head of Shambhala and reigns together with the Seven Kumaras — the Great Teachers, or the Masters of Wisdom, who personify the Seven Rays. Each era must be permeated with the energies of a particular Ray in whose Light the next stage of planetary evolution develops. And so for each period of time He designates one of the Mahatmas as the Ruler of Shambhala, who bears the titles of Maha-Chohan (*Sanskrit*, "Great Lord"), Rigden (*Tibetan*, "Holder of the Lineage"), and Kalki (*Sanskrit*, "Destroyer of Ignorance"). And the current time is referred to as the Era of the Heart, which is to bring about a Synthesis of all Seven Rays.

In 1924, Mahatma Serapis was replaced by Mahatma Morya in this momentous position. The Master of Helena Blavatsky and Helena Roerich became the Great Lord of Shambhala, changing His Name to Maitreya, for each era requires an affirmation of the power of a particular Name. This Great Lord is the 25th King of Shambhala — Rigden Dragpo Khorlocan (*Tibetan*, "Wielder of the Iron Wheel"), also known as Kalki Rudra Chakrin (*Sanskrit*, "Forceful Wheel Holder") — under whose reign, according to legend, the Great Battle of Armageddon was to be fought between the forces of Good — the Warriors of Shambhala — and the forces of evil. The Master M. is the Bearer of all Rays, who brings the synthesis of all the energies given to the world throughout the history of human civilization. He is the highest among the Seven Kumaras (or Gods), who, coming from the Distant Worlds, were responsible for the evolution of planet Earth. In other words, the Lord Morya and the Solar Hierarch constitute One Individuality, made manifest in both earthly and Heavenly forms.

The Puranas and other sacred texts state that it is from Shambhala, the City of Gods, that the Kalki Avatar would emerge to establish the Golden Age on Earth. The present Great King of Shambhala is the Messiah promised by all world religions: Christ of Christianity, Maitreya of Buddhism, Mahdi of Islam, Kalki of Hinduism, the Messiah of Judaism, Saoshyant of Zoroastrianism, Li Hong of Taoism, and so on.

IDEA — the true essence of thought, unexpressed in form; fore-thought. Thus, at first, an idea appears in consciousness, which clads itself in the matter of thought and develops into an image that then acquires material form (visible or invisible) and is embodied in life.

According to Cosmic Laws, which also exist beyond form (but are manifested in Primordial Matter), all phenomena unexpressed in form subordinate whatever is clad in form, and subsequently subordination takes place according to the degree of rarefaction in matter, with the physical degree being the lowest. Hence Plato was right when he stated that "Ideas rule the world." Ideas as such, unlike thoughts, are always invisible, even in the Higher Worlds.

The Great Teachers saturate space with the most advanced ideas. The birth of an idea calls forth the particles of consonant elements which act as a magnet, creating a field of attraction around it. So, an invisible search for allies apparently occurs among people who are willing to turn this idea into reality by using human hands and feet. The border between two ages, that is taking place now, is marked by a great penetration of new ideas into the depths of space in order to awaken dormant consciousness. And these ideas enter the consciousness of many, thereby dividing humanity into two camps: those who follow them, and those who counteract them. If one's consciousness is ready, it accepts the new ideas without difficulty. Those who follow evolution develop them — from different points of view — all over the world. But no barrier or restriction can keep them from spreading to all hearts and minds. Thus, ideas are borne through the air, compelling everyone to make a firm decision as to what they support: whether they are for peace or for war, for freedom or for slavery, for remaining in the old world or for entering the New World, and so on.

The published Teachings of Light represent thoughts expressed in words and gathered together in printed books. Many sections of the Secret Teachings remain unpublished and are contained in manuscripts stored at Shambhala and other Abodes of Light. But the larger portion is sealed in the archives of space, or Akasha, which is inaccessible to ordinary people. However, the Great Teachers have permeated space with thoughts that are in tune with the evolutionary stage reached by humanity to date. In this way, they share with the world what every sensitive spirit may perceive from the spheres surrounding Earth. Even in cases where the Teaching is not published, its ideas still fill space, as if borne through the air. They reach many hearts and, in different parts of the world, people begin to speak and express the same thoughts and espouse the same formulas, although they have never had contact with the Teaching on the physical plane. As they bring the light of heart-centredness into the world around them, they begin to facilitate the unification of humanity into a single family. In this way they prepare the ground for future change in the world, for the transformation of individual consciousness, as well as their whole life.

Ideas never die, but live in space, although they may be forgotten. But as time goes by, they once again spark interest in human minds and, as they increase in strength, they are embodied in life, even after thousands of years. And ideas that express indisputable truths are immortal, only changing the form of their manifestation simultaneous to the evolution of consciousness.

Naturally, progressive ideas are seldom accepted immediately. They generally require a period of time to take root in the consciousness of the masses. But as the majority become accustomed to them, accepting them as their own thoughts, these ideas begin to rule the world on a practical rather than a theoretical level.

INITIATE — one who has become entitled to acquire the Secret Knowledge of the Cosmos and human beings. Each new stage of Initiation reveals ever new mysteries and imparts new abilities.

Initiation ceremonies — or Mysteries — took place in Ancient Sanctuaries such as the Pyramids of Egypt, the Temples of Greece, India, and so on. Secret Sanctuaries with halls for Initiations were built in places of powerful energy, mostly in the mountains. Mountains are the source of the strongest energy because their summits are covered with snow, which, like a natural lens, serves to receive the currents of other constellations and planets. Similarly, representatives of other worlds who study the Earth have their bases in the mountains, too.

The procedure of Initiation is a mystical penetration into a higher level of perception and comprehension of the mystery of Existence, thanks to the acceptance of higher-order currents and the ability to use them effectively. It is the transition from life to a temporary death by means of a magic dream, which in turn enables a candidate to experience a disembodied Spirit and Soul in the subjective world. Each Initiation requires moral purity, strength of spirit, and an aspiration towards Truth.

For example, Hermes Trismegistus (*Greek*, "Thrice-Greatest") underwent three Initiations, although he is already the Four-time-Greatest, having successfully passed through yet another. His father, Arraim, is a Four-time-Greatest also. Thales of Argos passed through four Initiations. Christ passed through Eight Initiations, and His Second Coming is associated with His Ninth Initiation.

However, it is not only people and the Great Spirits who may go through Initiations, but also realms of Nature, planets, stars, solar systems, etc. Thus, in the present day, humanity as a whole as well as Earth are undergoing the next level of their Fiery Initiation.

KARMA (*Sanskrit*, "action") — Cosmic Law of Cause and Effect, expressed in the formula, "as you sow, so shall you reap"; defines the limits within which the destiny of an individual, people, or planet, and so on can be developed.

Karma neither punishes nor rewards; it is simply a single Universal Law that infallibly guides all other laws, producing certain effects in accordance with corresponding causes. Every word, action, thought, or desire leads to an appropriate effect — and, eventually, to everything in one's surroundings. Nothing happens accidentally. Karma may be individual and collective, embracing whole peoples, continents, planets, and star systems. One cannot change or eliminate it except by removing the causes that underlie human actions.

Every individual bears the mark of karmic predestination from birth. Their free will is determined by the limits dictated by Karma, which is in turn created by their own human will. However, the placing of obstacles and restrictions in one area opens up opportunities in another. The purpose of Karma is to direct all humankind towards the path of Evolution.

Karmic debts are formed when an individual's free will violates the Divine Laws set forth in all world religions in various forms. Ignorance of these Laws does not exempt the individual from bearing responsibility. This may not happen immediately. It can take several incarnations before a person is offered the opportunity to pay off the karmic debts that they have accumulated, through the creation of certain conditions. The fastest way to redeem karma is to show Love to all, especially to those who wish you ill. Those who have succeeded in paying off 51% of their debts receive the opportunity to cooperate with Higher Forces.

The age of 42 years — 24 years for future generations — is considered the age of "cosmic adulthood." At this age begins the *Karma of Love*, when people are to work with the Cosmos on a spiritual level: for example, helping others by sharing their life experiences or developing some spiritual quality within themselves. Of course, they live on. But it also happens that, after the age of 42, some suffer a heart attack and pass on. This is because before reaching the age of 42 they needed to fulfil a certain programme associated with their former Karma. Once the soul completes its task, it brings about a new incarnation. Or vice versa: a human spirit may realize that its present body is unable to perform a certain divine task and, so as not to waste time, attempts to weave together another body. Thus, as is evident, once they reach the age of 40 most people begin to take an interest in spiritual practices and ponder their mission in life — this is the Cosmic Karma of Love coming into effect. However, the Karma of Love may touch not only a human life but also the life of humanity as a whole, within smaller or greater evolutionary cycles.

Lavra (*Greek*, "alley") — monastery of the highest rank in the Eastern Orthodox Church.

Lhasa (*Tibetan*) — the capital of Tibet. Derived from the word Lha meaning "Spirits of the Highest Spheres."

Mahatma (*Sanskrit*, "Great Soul") — Adept of the highest order. The term designates exalted beings who, having attained full mastery over their lower natures, are in possession of extraordinary knowledge and power commensurate with the stage they have reached in their spiritual evolution. After leaving the world of humanity, they return to their native planets as Radiant Gods.

Maitreya Sangha[1] (*Sanskrit*, "Community of Maitreya") — Sign of Maitreya; Sign of the Era of Love; Sign of the Heart. Also denotes the network of invisible Abodes of the Great Teachers, which are spread out high up in the Himalayas, encircling the Chief Stronghold, where the Temple of the Lord of Shambhala is located.

The square is a sacred figure, being a symbol of immortality. This is also a Pyramid, because the Pyramid stands on a quadrangular foundation and ends with a point at the top, thus representing a triad and a quadrangle, or numbers 3 and 4. The square is the geometric expression of moral justice and divine balance.

Helena Roerich's notebooks also contain the explanation that the square was a symbol of her Teaching in one of her past lives.

---

[1] Appears as the symbol on the cover of this book.

Masters of Wisdom — Great Teachers of Humanity, who have taken responsibility for its evolution. Through suffering and sacrifice, Masters of Wisdom are those who have achieved a high level of development, far surpassing that of the ordinary individual — and, of course, in the human understanding, they can be seen as Gods. In the 19th and early 20th centuries, six Mahatmas were incarnated, known under the following names: Morya, Koot Hoomi, Rakoczy, Serapis, Hilarion, and Djual Khool. Now they no longer occupy their former physical bodies, and they have also changed their names; some have gone on to other, more advanced planets, leaving worthy earthly successors in their place.

The Masters are the Great Guardians of Truth, who implement the Divine Plan. They know when, what, and how much should be given to people and attentively watch over their evolution. There is so much intense work that the Mahatmas have no time for anything personal. They create new causes that bring about the effects needed for Evolution, thereby helping humanity to liquidate its former Karma. They know in advance the flow of consequences and can project them for millennia ahead. And sometimes, when the Teachers foresee the future, they know the effects of the causes consciously produced by them. So, they create the future, which is pliant in the hands of their fiery will. The Masters know the course of the stars and their future combinations and coordinate their creative work with the energies of the Cosmos.

One of the most essential tasks of the Great Brotherhood is the selection and guidance of colleagues and disciples. For various reasons, the Teachers cannot enter into direct and close contact with multitudes of people. They act through their colleagues, disciples, and messengers. When their disciples are incarnated on Earth with a definite mission, the Masters follow and guide them from childhood. The karmic relationship of many millennia enables the Teachers to make contact with their disciples without difficulty. In addition to being taught secret sciences, they usually undergo a fiery transmutation that allows them to maintain communication with the Masters. The disciples are constantly being tested, even at higher levels of development. The most terrible betrayals are also unavoidable in their lives.

Each century, the Mahatmas admit into their Abodes of Light a maximum of two candidates to convey through them a part of the Secret Knowledge. But for various reasons this may not always be necessary. The chief consideration is that the messenger's body must be ready to receive the Teaching. The Teachings of Light, of course, never appear spontaneously — there are specific periods allotted to them. To record the Teaching, the disciples go through many incarnations of preparation, sometimes for thousands of years, and when the time comes, they are alerted beforehand to the work they are about to undertake. As a rule, preliminary preparation takes place over three years, during which time the Higher Spirits work with the disciples, attuning their bodies.

Contrary to established opinion, the Great Teachers do not make contact with mediums or channellers, except in very rare cases, and when they do, it is usually through their advanced disciples.

It must be remembered that on turning towards the Powers of Light, a person must initially establish a connection with their higher bodies: for example, the mental body will be higher than the emotional body, and the spirit can act as a Guide for the soul, as well as take on the role of god in relation to the body. And only after establishing a harmonious order of all seven bodies can a person hope that someone from Above will pay attention to them, according to their vibrational sound, or Karma, both human and spiritual, depending on the goal they set for themselves, or that was set by Teachers who entrusted them with a specific mission.

Helena Blavatsky had to accept the body of a powerful medium, which was necessary for the tasks assigned to her during her final life on Earth. She was required to work with many people and perform miracles to convince them of the existence of the higher Laws of Nature and Supreme Knowledge. Nevertheless, with the help of her Master, she brought her ability under complete control. Before revealing *The Secret Doctrine* to humanity, Blavatsky experienced the fiery transmutation of her body for three years under the supervision of her Teacher in one of His Ashrams in Tibet. For those who have endured this process, it is tough to be out in the world amongst people, and all the more so amongst those adversely disposed towards them. This was the reason for Blavatsky's poor health. Helena Roerich went through something similar and even more intense when she received *Agni Yoga*. However, she lived in India in the pure mountain air in almost total solitude, surrounded by loving individuals, conditions that enabled her to almost wholly accomplish the mission of her last earthly incarnation.

Initially, when the Leaders of Humanity first came into the world, the continents were divided into seven spheres, wherein each of the Great Lords emitted their own luminous vibrations. As the rainbow is dispersed into seven colours, so all the Seven Great Teachers represent the Seven Rays, bringing with them the currents consonant with their particular note. At the present time, each of the Seven Masters of Wisdom has educated disciples who have reached a high level of consciousness. The precise number of the Leaders of Humanity is now 777. Naturally, each of these Teachers also has their own Teacher, for the process of cognition is limitless.

In essence, the Seven Great Teachers — the Seven Rays — are the components of the One Supreme Lord, who represents the White Ray and personifies the Spiritual Sun. Thus, there is One Individuality, but His partial manifestations enlightened such earthly incarnations as Buddha, Christ, Maitreya, and other Great Teachers.

MAYA (*Sanskrit*, "illusion") — illusive and transient nature of earthly reality and existence.

OCCULTISM (*Latin*, "hidden," "secret") — the totality of sciences that study spiritual forces in human beings and the Cosmos, as well as the unfathomed properties of matter and consciousness.

PSYCHIC ENERGY — primary fiery energy that lies at the foundation of the manifested world.

RAY — creative power, energy; the focused Fire of space that creates and constructs all visible and invisible forms of life on all planes of existence. A ray is a material body, a form of the expression of Light, stretching out through space in all directions and saturated with the subtlest substance of matter, containing a myriad of electrons. Ray energy is creative, for it carries elements which both combine among themselves and form compounds with elements of other rays by the Law of Magnetism and Consonance, thereby generating new types and combinations of matter and various orders of phenomena, along with whole new worlds. Thus, invisible and visible rays are mighty producers and movers of life, regulating the life of each specific organism and form.

The influence of the rays of the Sun and stars extends to all that exists on Earth. Life has always depended on celestial bodies, for its elements are to be found in the Universe. Rays of energy from the celestial bodies are sent to Earth for the combination and generation of new forms. Hence the rays of every planet take part in constructing each individual's physical body, the various elements of which are scattered throughout cosmic space among the corresponding stars. At a person's birth the rays intersect and develop the framework within which their physical, astral, and mental bodies are constructed. The form of each organ — heart, lungs, liver, etc. — depends on the combination of rays from corresponding stars at the moment of birth. The alignment of the stars is always precisely determined and may be calculated for any given moment. Human beings are a concentration of the influence of rays, having gathered crystals of cosmic energies in the seed of their spirit for billions of years. The rays of the celestial bodies and their combinations condition not only the life of each individual, but also that of whole peoples, planets, star systems, and so on.

The solar ray bears the essence of the structure and chemical composition of the Sun along with charges of powerful electromagnetic energy — bipolar in essence, threefold in manifestation, septenary in structure, and duodecimal in tonality. The visible solar ray is just one of its basest manifestations. The invisible rays of the solar spectrum, of course, are not limited to ultraviolet and infrared rays, but stretch out on both sides of the visible scale. This ray essence is natural not only to the rays of the Sun, but also to any star and to any centre of existence in either an actual or a potential state. And if the heart is the Sun of the body, then, consequently, every heart possesses the same qualities in its inexhaustible potential. Thus, everything radiates light, but that light varies in terms of substance and degree.

Each Ray is a personified Being on any given plane of Existence, and every evolving person is a particle of a given Ray. By this analogy, one may assume that the One White Ray of Sirius is personified by its Planetary Spirit, known as Sanat Kumara, the Lord of Civilization. On reaching the Solar System, this Ray refracts into the White Solar Ray that represents the Solar Hierarch, who is made manifest as the Great Masculine Principle called Christ or Maitreya, while the Great

Feminine Principle is the Mother of the World or Sophia. That is, Sanat Kumara is Father to both Christ and Sophia. The Solar Hierarch in His trichotomy manifests as Buddha, Christ, and Maitreya (or as Brahma, Vishnu, and Shiva), while Sophia manifests as Faith, Hope, and Love. The septenary nature of the Ray is expressed in the Seven Great Teachers, each of which personifies one of the Seven Rays, symbolizing the mastery of the corresponding stratum or type of matter. And each Teacher has a Spiritual Sister.

All the Lords pour the Light of their Rays into the world. They also use the Rays to communicate with their disciples. Every disciple is assigned a certain shade of their Master's Ray, through which they receive knowledge and information directly from Him. In this way, the Ray serves as a special tool for the translation of impenetrable Cosmic Knowledge into something that the disciple's consciousness is capable of perceiving. In addition this helps to prevent gross distortions of Truth, since anyone can access the Ocean of Knowledge, but only a few are able to understand it and convey it correctly to others.

The current Era of Maitreya is the Era of the Synthesis of all Seven Rays, which together constitute the Colour White, but every two thousand years, a certain Ray, associated with one of the Seven Lords, dominates. Thus, the Ray of Christ has prevailed for two thousand years — the Age of Pisces. The next two thousand years will be the Age of Aquarius of the Master Rakoczy, also known as Saint-Germain, the Lord of the Seventh Ray. So, now the Violet Ray makes its appearance, alongside the White Ray.

Of course, here one cannot use the concept of *Time*, as it is Cycles that prevail. The process of Transfiguration began in 1942, when esoterically the Age of Aquarius came into force. However, it is impossible to pinpoint the precise moment at which one thing ends and another thing begins, because everything crosses over in a gradual flow. For a while, the two Eras will overlap. Nevertheless, the Age of Aquarius is gathering momentum with every passing day.

The numbering of the Rays varies according to different traditions; if viewed from the point of view of energy centres (chakras), then the first colour is red and it starts with Kundalini (in the coccyx region) and ascends up the spinal column. But if one starts at Sahasrara (the crown), then this — the violet ray is regarded as the first. The gradation of the Rays also differs. There are Rays of the Solar Systems, such as the Ray of Reason (emerald in colour), which dominated the First Solar System; the Second Ray of Love-Wisdom is now being manifested (rarefied rose in colour), and the next Solar System will be dominated by the First Ray of Will and Power (white in colour). Also, each of the Seven Great Lords is the carrier of Rays of a certain colour, and these also have their own series of numbering and gradation.

The sciences of the future, such as astrology, astrochemistry, astrobiology, astrophysiology, and astrophysics, will reveal the secrets of rays.

SENZAR — the language of the Sun based on symbolism and closely associated with Sound, Light, Colour, and Number. Currently, Senzar is the secret sacerdotal language of the Great Teachers and their disciples all over the world. It is taught in the Secret Schools of the East.

In the ancient past there was one body of knowledge and one universal language — Senzar. From the beginning of human evolution, these were transmitted from generation to generation. Yet during the times of Atlantis, when humanity fell into sin, this language, along with eternal knowledge, ceased to be available to posterity. All nations restricted themselves to their own national tongues and lost their connection with the Secret Wisdom, forgetting the one language. Humanity was no longer worthy of such knowledge. So, instead of being universal, Senzar became limited to just a few. The biblical myth of the Tower of Babel and similar legends around the world symbolically testify to that enforced secrecy, narrating the story when the Lord created several languages from the one original language, so that sinners could no longer understand one another's speech. In mythology Senzar is often referred to as the language of the birds.

The tongues of all peoples through the ages have their origins in Senzar. Thus, the roots of many current eastern languages come from Sanskrit, which is based on Senzar. Many words of this most ancient language underlie not only Sanskrit but also Egyptian, Hebrew, Latin, and other languages of various known and yet-to-be discovered sacred texts. Thus, Senzar is similar to the roots that nourish a single Tree, and languages compose its crown which is beautiful in its diversity.

The language of Senzar consists of many levels, having both spoken and written forms of speech, which are significantly different from traditional understanding. It is also distinct from others in that it has no obsolete or ingrained forms of expression. Being rather succinct, it is able to most fully and concisely express any thought, including hugely sophisticated phenomena.

Its highest manifestations are closest to the Voice of Silence and include thought-forms, the breathing of fires, the geometric expression of combinations of rays, and so on — whereas its lowest manifestations resemble traditional writing systems, each with its own specific rules.

The writing system of Senzar combines seemingly incompatible elements. These include signs, syllables, and letters based on symbolism. A single symbol is capable of developing into an entire treatise, easily comprehended by an initiated disciple of any ethnic background. But the reader's level of consciousness is also important. Colour, light, number, and sound play a significant role in its alphabet from which words and sentences are composed. Each letter, possessing its own specific colour of the rainbow, shade of light, number, and mystic sound syllable, has its equivalent in the languages of all peoples of the world and may be reproduced using different cryptographic methods with the aid of specialized calculation tables. Thus, a new cryptographic alphabet is created in a given tongue while numerological, geometrical, and astrological keys help the reader to precisely determine how to decode this secret writing system.

For example, the Angelic language of John Dee, mysterious advisor to Queen Elizabeth I, is *one version* of script in the Senzar language.

In present times, Senzar has been discovered in inscriptions on stones and plants that do not lend themselves to deciphering. For example, on the territory of the Buddhist monastery Kumbum in China grows the sacred Tree of Great Merit, also known as the Tree of Ten Thousand Images. Legend has it that the tree grew out of the hair of the great Buddhist reformer Tsongkhapa. In the past, according to witnesses,[1] when the tree blossomed, on each leaf there appeared a sacred letter or syllable of such astounding beauty and perfection that no other existing letter could surpass it. These mystic letters and syllables were written in Senzar, and in their totality comprised the whole Teaching of Buddhism and the history of the world.

SHAMBHALA (*Sanskrit*, "Place of Peace") — Stronghold of Light, legendary kingdom hidden in the heart of the Himalayas. The Kingdom figures under different names in the myths and beliefs of various peoples of the world: Agartha, Belovodye, the City of Gods, the Garden of Eden, Mount Meru,

---

[1] See Évariste Huc, *Travels in Tartary, Thibet, and China, 1844–1846*, vol. 2 (London: Office of the National Illustrated Library, 1852), pp. 52–54.

the Pure Land, the White Island, and so on. Shambhala is the Imperishable Sacred Land, the first and ever-present continent of the planet Earth, which never shared the fate of the others, for it is destined to continue from the beginning to the end of the Grand Cycle of Evolution. It is the cradle of the first human and contains the sacral Source of all religions, philosophies, sciences, and esoteric teachings. This mysterious place, which preserves the Eternal Wisdom, lies at the intersection of the past, present, and future, as well as the Physical, Subtle, and Fiery Worlds.

Shambhala was first mentioned in the Puranas. Information related to it filtered into the world at different times. In the 17th century, the Portuguese Jesuit missionary, Estêvão Cacella, was the first to tell the Europeans of this mythical place, which he visited at the invitation of the Tibetans. In 1915, Albert Grünwedel published a German translation of the Guidebook to Shambhala, written by the famous Panchen Lama, Lobsang Palden Yeshe in which the location of the legendary realm is indicated by a large number of symbols and complex geographical hints. And in 1925, in many newspapers worldwide, there appeared an extensive article by the Mongolian explorer, Dr. Lao Chin, telling of his journey to the Valley of Shambhala. Although he was forbidden to write about the wondrous spiritual phenomena of the place, Dr. Lao Chin mentioned that the valley's inhabitants lived for many centuries despite looking middle-aged, and that they were characterized by clairvoyance, telepathy, and other higher abilities. Among other things, Dr. Chin witnessed them levitating, even becoming invisible to the naked eye.[1]

Shambhala is the Ashram of the Great Brotherhood of the Teachers of Humanity, each of whom is a God, having become such for many nations, leaving the divine mark in human

---

[1] To read Dr. Lao Chin's article about his journey to one of the Abodes of Shambhala, visit radiantbooks.co/bonus.

hearts as an equal among equals in the flesh. The work of the Mahatmas may be seen in three principal areas of research: improvement of the earthly plane, methods of communication with the Distant Worlds, and means of conveying the results of their study to humanity, the latter being undoubtedly the most challenging.

Earthly Shambhala may be thought of as a spaceport from which messengers are sent to the Distant Worlds and where ambassadors from the infinite Universe arrive. New ideas from other inhabited planets are tested in the laboratories of the Brotherhood; after being adapted to earthly conditions, they are conveyed to the world's scientists in the form of inspiration.

Here the most important decisions concerning the evolution of humanity and the planet are made. The Council of Shambhala convenes once in every hundred years (1924, 2024); the Council of the High Initiates takes place once every sixty years. This is a real World Government, which has little in common with earthly regimes, and yet has often contacted them through its messengers. Indeed, the history of all times and nations records testimonies to the Assistance of the Great Teachers, which has always been secretly given at turning points in the history of every country. However, while the people of the East often accepted their advice, the West, as a rule, rejected them.

Several prominent individuals have visited Shambhala. As a rule, one or two candidates are admitted each "century" (which consists not of a hundred years but of sixty, in accordance with the Kalachakra Calendar). For example, during their lifetimes, this Stronghold of Light was visited by: Gautama Buddha, Jesus Christ, Lao-Tzu, Pythagoras, Plato, Apollonius of Tyana, Paracelsus, the Panchen Lama Palden Yeshe, Helena Blavatsky, Helena and Nicholas Roerich, and others — all of whom have played a significant role in the evolution of humanity. But not all the Great Spirits who had specific missions to fulfil visited the Brotherhood during their earthly life. Furthermore, anyone who visits this Abode of Light by the invitation that resonates deep within their heart, takes a vow of silence, which may be broken only with the permission of the Great Lord of Shambhala. No uninvited guest will ever find the path to Shambhala.

SPACE — just like Time, an indispensable condition for evolution, the cognition of Existence, and testing of the true qualities of one living creature or another.

The more subtle and higher the matter, the less the importance of Space and Time. Thus, in the Higher Worlds, space has no distance, and the human spirit may be in different places at the same time.

TACTICA ADVERSA (*Latin*, "adverse") — a reverse tactic, which ensures success for the Forces of Light in the worst of conditions, i.e., it enables them to derive benefit from negative circumstances.

TEACHING OF LIFE — totality of all the Teachings of Light that the Great Teachers have continuously poured upon Earth from time immemorial to the present day. This includes all known sacred texts such as the Vedas, the Avesta, the Tripitaka, the Bible, and the Quran, as well as *The Secret Doctrine*, *Teachings of the Temple*, *Agni Yoga*, and *The Teaching of the Heart*.

THOUGHT — Fire, or fiery energy, clothed by the will in material form of a certain level of firmness and durability, while striving to become realized. Thought-forms can be seen by powerful clairvoyants and they can also be registered using scientific methods. The outer layer of any thought is invisibly linked to its creator. It becomes endowed by a person's will with a certain magnetic force.

Thought is the basis of everything that exists in the Universe. Thought is limited by neither time nor space; its power knows no bounds. Still, it is restricted by Cosmic Law. Therefore, every thought that has ever been generated — even thousands of years ago in previous lives, must sooner or later become manifest in action.

Since the nature of thought is subtle and fiery rather than physical — meaning that it is a higher energy that subordinates all lower energies to its power — it can shape the physical world around a person. So, thought produces an image which is consolidated and encased in the flesh of the Subtle World, and is then embodied on Earth as some sort of consequence, appearing in the corresponding form of matter. But for this purpose, it must have a clear and distinct image, which endues it with the appropriate strength and shape to overcome the limits of Time necessary for it to be manifested in the material world. Moreover, a person must work to create the necessary conditions. The magnetic power of thought attracts kindred and consonant elements from space on the principle of "like attracts like," growing like a snowball. Thus a thought that has been sent into space is still linked to its owner, and periodically returns to this person for affirmation or negation, moving like a boomerang. A thought can revolve, like a comet, around the one who put the initial bundle of energy into it, and that energy determines the corresponding radius and orbit of revolution. If the person does not reject it, and continues to make an effort to realize it, their will endows it with new force, and it again goes out into space, increasing the radius of its influence, and so on until the thought becomes a reality, having received sufficient energy from both its creator and the surrounding environment. On the other hand, if at any point the person begins to doubt the thought or no longer needs it, and they stop applying the effort required for its realization, then the thought loses its force, gradually weakens, and eventually breaks down into primary elements, never revealing its potential. At the same time, creating a strong, clear thought and then forgetting about it completely does not equate to destroying it. The thought will again return to its producer and will eventually come to realization, possibly many centuries later. Thoughts and dreams always come true when environmental conditions and the composition of its elements favour their manifestation, not necessarily at the time or in the way that people anticipate.

From this one can imagine how huge conglomerates of different thoughts generated by humankind, like a giant storm or bank of luminous clouds, hang over the heads of various individuals. The thoughts that appear suddenly may gladden or upset them. Or a thought may push them to take their own life or to harm another being. Here it is for each to decide whether they will take an aggressive path and increase the destructive force, or respond with a prayer whose luminous power will bring albeit a tiny spark of light into the surrounding pitch-black darkness, thereby helping light-bearing conglomerates in space to grow.

Due to their energetic nature, thoughts are subject to the Supreme Laws discussed in all the sacred scriptures. The Supreme Laws are also energies that govern the entire Universe, but they are even higher in power, and therefore, all others submit to them, and to change this is beyond the power of human beings.

Thus, dark thoughts are doomed to perdition by the power of Cosmic Law, and since they are all connected to their creators, they pull these individuals after them. In contrast, thoughts of light are eternal and can grow infinitely, giving spiritual ascent to their originators. Thoughts directed towards oneself soar close to that person, illuminating or darkening their consciousness, depending on their nature. It is scientifically proven that thoughts expressed in words affect water and plants, and therefore it is not difficult to continue this pattern and assume that they affect the human body and soul in precisely the same way. Evil and negative thoughts will destroy a person's vital force, serving as the cause of various diseases. But one should bear in mind that on the whole illnesses are categorized as *admitted* (due to ruinous actions and habits), *karmic* (as an unpaid debt from a past life), and *sacred* (as a result of a Fiery or planetary experiment). And vice versa: positive, optimistic, and joyful thoughts imbue the organism with the energies of life, increasing them in both the person and the space that surrounds them.

Thought creates a person's internal appearance, which to a certain extent is reflected in the physical body. Thus we are the reflection of our thoughts, and eventually we become what and who we want to be. Consequently, thought is an instrument for the self-perfection (or involution) of human beings. Similarly, the collective thought of humanity powerfully affects the living conditions of the planet, making them better or worse depending on the common nature of thought.

It is generally accepted that thoughts are generated by the brain. Yet, in modern language, the brain can be likened to a physical computer that is only able to perceive our thoughts that are created on the invisible levels of human nature, both low and high, and to project them onto our physical senses of perception. An individual does not lose the ability to think if they lose the physical body. However, it is not only the brain that can perceive thought: so too can the heart. It is the heart that receives the thoughts produced by our higher centres of consciousness, and only then does it transmit them to the brain for registration, often as flashes of intuition. Thus, the currents of thought passing through the heart are much more effective than those that pass through the brain and bypass the heart, because the heart imbues them with a special kind of energy that will help them overcome any obstacle. In this way, thought can be governed by two centres: the brain and the heart — each in its own way, using particular types of energy of varying degrees of subtlety. Currents of thought sent by the heart are especially effective; the thoughts of the brain are much weaker, and have a much shorter radius of action.

Thoughts can protect a person, certain places, and objects, as well as help another, uniting instantly with the object of aspiration. Their effect may last for a long or a short time, depending on the assigned period or volitional order. They may also have an accurately defined and strictly limited purpose. Everything depends on the strength of the heart energy or fire that is put into these currents. The most powerful thoughts are those created by the Power of Love — in fact, they are able to create entire worlds.

For example, the infamous "curse of the pharaohs" is a consequence of the fact that the objects belonging to the kings came long under the protection afforded by high priests with the help of thought. These objects of the past have a special energy and aura that have been in a state of harmony for considerable lengths of time. When scientists disturb the peace of the pharaohs' tombs, they do so without controlling their thoughts, and so what happens is that their thoughts of profit or worldly fame, which represent low forms of energy, add dissonance, as though breaking a sacred protective net that was defending not only the mummified body of the pharaoh, but his tomb, together with all the items placed inside. And as a rule, in the case of a pharaoh who has passed certain degrees of Initiation, the protection is multi-level. In this matter, the focus should be on the invisible planes, because here, just as in Nature, the absolute heterogeneity of mental energies causes an invisible tornado, which lifts up dangerous microscopic particles that are then inhaled by those who have disturbed the pharaoh's peace. The result can manifest in the form of a deadly disease.

Discipline of thought is the principal condition for progress. Because of the concept of *Time* in the dense world, a certain period is required before the consequences of anything become apparent. But in the Higher Worlds, time no longer has this power, therefore thoughts become a reality instantly, and people reap the fruits of the thoughts they produced during their lives on Earth. It is important now to learn how to control our thoughts so as to avoid creating additional problems for ourselves in the Subtle World.

The science of thought is the science of the future. Mastery of thought will lead to the mastery of many secrets of Nature and to the achievement of the might of spirit.

URUSVATI (*Sanskrit*, "Light of the Morning Star") — spiritual name given by the Great Teachers to Helena Roerich.

WORD — an outer layer of thought; its seeming physical form, regardless of whether it is expressed as sound or symbol. Word is inseparable from thought, which means that it is a carrier of Fire, either bright or dark. Hence every phrase uttered carries an energy component, which can be saturated with both poisonous fumes and life-saving currents — each word contains within itself either a constructive or a destructive power. The World was created by the Word. Therefore, the word is a powerful force, if used conscientiously.

Each letter, by virtue of its vibrational key, affects the human nervous system through its corresponding vibrations. Not only that, but it also awakens as yet unmanifested forces in space. Vowel sounds are fiery in nature, while consonants are perishable and earthly. Indeed, one can evoke healing energies from space through a particular combination of vowel sounds, whereas the low-frequency, hiss consonants are capable of causing rockslides, tornadoes, and other destructive phenomena, including earthquakes. Also, every word spoken represents fiery energy — transmitted, or radiated, by the body through the mouth. The affected nerves flare up like wires with fiery currents and cause an external flash in the form of fiery formations. Words fly through space like colourful balls of fire. Every letter creates fiery discharges. Even ordinary conversation can be imagined as an exchange of fires or coloured rays. Thought encased in words is cast into the surrounding sphere, and either remains there, influencing the environment long after the words are spoken and forgotten, or flies to its destination.

Words are the channels for the magnetic attraction from space of what their essence expresses. None of the energies, once put into action, disappear completely; each brings forth its own consequences, depending on its nature and especially its producer, for the crystal of such energy remains in their aura. Thus, these energies are forever connected to their creator by a magnetic thread. They are their spatial property, which will not leave them until the magnetic force of these words is exhausted. The energies again return to their producer in order to be neutralized, in order that the disturbed balance might be restored. Hence one must be accountable for every word one utters. The dense conditions of the earthly plane often prevent the completion of this process, but after death, the process of neutralizing one's own created energies continues freely and unhindered in the Subtle World, until it consumes everything — bad or good — that one has generated on Earth.

Since words are external symbols of the thoughts behind them, the repetition of any word calls into being the latent energy within it, and this affects the person and the space around them. Even the mental repetition of words which affirm high and positive qualities is beneficial. In this way, through words we may bring ourselves and others into a harmonious or an inharmonious state. The power of verbal prayer, for example, has been known since ancient times.

The mystery of perfection in speech and text lies in the absolute harmony of form and content. The vibrational keys of words, their sound and tonality, the colour of the thoughts concealed in them, should be in full consonance and harmony. Provided there is such an accord, spoken and written texts can be expressed in any rhythm and tonality. Words can be short and abrupt if the rhythm so requires, and sentences may feature peculiar constructions, since the power of influence resides not in the external form, but in the consonance between the words and the essence expressed therein. A properly and harmoniously constructed rhythm of speech or text has a tremendous invisible impact. This is why the creations of some writers and poets are considered to be great, and why some scriptures are held as sacred.

For the reasons cited above, all Teachings emphasize *discipline* in word and speech. After all, it is better to be silent than to experience the blows of spatial energy upon ourselves. Silence is golden: we do not squander our precious fiery energy in vain. Many people are sick because they waste their strength through their own talkativeness. Besides, great harm is done by idle chatter when one should really remain silent. For example, if one has made an important decision or special plans, one should not advertise this to anyone prematurely, since disembodied evil entities populating the near-Earth space may overhear it and do everything in their power to hinder these plans. It is easier to hide thoughts than words from subtle beings, for not all disembodied entities are capable of mind-reading.

Moreover, foul language is inadmissible, being the antipode of prayer. Everyone is familiar with the phrase "words can kill," and we must be aware that anyone who promotes death kills themselves and their soul, first and foremost. Scientists have already discovered that "impure words" uttered with a loud or quiet voice (or even a whisper) have equally destructive effects on the living cells of our body. Therefore, instead of antipodal words, it is important to produce pure, light phrases that will help both those who utter them and the surrounding space.

In the future, humanity will no longer send shockwaves into space through the sounds of its speech. Instead, communication will be mental, or telepathic. Until then, we should be careful in our use of the great power of the word and employ it only for the good. It is worth attempting to follow the wise precept of Christ: "But let your communication be, Yea, yea; Nay, nay: for whatsoever is more than these cometh of evil."

WORLDS — various states, or planes, of Cosmic Matter. For the present Solar System, there exist Seven Worlds, each of which has seven sub-planes, according to the degree of rarefaction and refinement.

In the current Fourth Round of Evolution, Four Worlds are available to humanity and Earth:

1. *The Physical World*, *the Dense World*, or *the Material World* — The Earth itself on which physical humanity lives.

2. *The Subtle World*, *the Ethereal World*, or *the Astral World* — This is the world where everyone goes during sleep. It exists in spheres encircling Earth, and its dimensions are much larger than the earthly plane. It consists of many layers, from the lowest to the highest, to which each individual is drawn by consonance. All individuals assume an appearance corresponding to their inner essence, and reap what they have sown on Earth. Its matter is pliant and instantly becomes an expression of what the spirit is thinking, and who that individual really is. Everything is created and moved by thought. Illumination occurs on account of the radiation of a person's subtle bodies, hence the lower spheres to which evil-minded people are drawn are dark. All earthly emotions and habits remain and assume a significantly intensified state. So if

a person has not overcome their most primitive desires on Earth, here they will suffer from the absence of a physical body through which to satisfy them. The lower areas of the Subtle World are the closest to Earth. Therefore, those in this layer often use Earth-dwellers to satisfy their desires — hence the phenomena of possession. For good people, not bound by physical passions, the Subtle World provides limitless freedom of spirit; here they can fly, endlessly create, contemplate creativity in all areas of life, and study and explore anything they wish. Souls may remain in this world for thousands of years.

3. **The Mental World**, or **the World of Thoughts** — Consists of the product of the mental creativity of thinking beings: mental forms or thought-forms. Its layers are determined by the affinity of thought emanations that comprise the content of the form. The line of attraction is determined by the attunement of one's consciousness. The process of attunement may take place subconsciously, but it can also take place by order of individual will. In this case the will chooses the point of attunement and establishes the necessary control. Whereas on Earth people travel by car, train, etc., in the Mental World they travel in the vehicle of thought. Consciousness enters thought like a passenger enters a railway carriage, and the vehicle of thought carries it to the sphere chosen by the mind.

4. **The Fiery World**, **the Empyreal World**, or **the Spiritual World** — Matter belonging to this world is so subtle, perfect and imbued with energy that it everywhere causes a fiery luminosity, hence its name. Here neither time nor distance exists in the earthly sense; everything happens "here and now." The beauty of this world is magnificent. The flowers are especially striking, and they are everywhere; they move and flutter, giving off marvellous fragrances and melodies. The elevated forms of matter and energy of which this world is comprised create an atmosphere of Joy and Love. However, not everyone is able to reach the Fiery World, because in order to do so they

must have developed their immortal fiery body. This happens when the individual follows a spiritual path on Earth.

When the Worlds are listed, the Mental World is often omitted. It serves as the living link between the Subtle and Fiery Worlds, belonging more to the latter, as thought cannot exist without Fire. Hence one might come across statements to the effect that there are *Three Worlds* accessible to humanity, and that the Fiery World is the World of Thought and vice versa.

The planet Earth exists in all these Worlds, and it is represented in each of them by its corresponding globe-sphere. All Four Worlds are combined concentrically one inside the other, forming the complex septenary body of the planet. Thus, Earth consists of dense physical matter, penetrated by spheres of subtle and fiery matter. All Seven Spheres of the planet in the Four Worlds are inhabited. Those who dwell in one World cannot see or sense the other Worlds. But they are continually moving from one World to another; dying in one, they are reborn in another, moving either upwards to the next higher planes or downwards once more to Earth. In this way, people pass through the Round of incarnations within the Planetary Chain.

Each of the consecutive bodies in which a person lives a conscious and full life, is restricted by the world and sphere to which it belongs, and is subject to its laws. All the Worlds have their boundaries and limitations, restricting people in some measure by the properties of matter. All ancient Teachings prescribed certain norms of behaviour, diets, and so on, aimed at the purification, or refinement, of the matter of all human bodies. The crude astral body, weighed down by crude habits, cannot rise higher than the lower layers of the Astral World, which are in perfect correlation to the composition of the astral body. Having been released from the dense body, only individuals that have purified their subtle bodies from dense particles on Earth can succeed in soaring high. In the Subtle World each disembodied person undergoes a process of cleansing, and yet, for all that, they cannot ascend higher than the height they themselves have attained. The Law of Consonance is just and infallible.

The planet Earth has already passed the lowest point — or greatest density — of its evolution, and so is now on a course of ascent. As a result, a convergence of the Dense and Subtle Worlds is gradually taking place, and the planet is rising one step higher than before. Hence the Subtle World is advancing on the Dense World, expanding the spheres of its own influence, thanks to the addition of properties that rarefy the matter of Earth; the Physical World, in turn, is harmoniously flowing into the layers of the Subtle Spheres. Similarly, the planet's Subtle World in its higher layers blends with the Mental World, and the Fiery World ascends into an even Higher World. Thus, in the Fifth Round, Five Worlds will be accessible to the Earth and humanity, where the Physical World will resemble the lowest layer of the Subtle World — that is, without the sharp demarcation between the two that is evident at the present time.

YUGA (*Sanskrit*, "age") — epoch, or cycle of Evolution, in Hinduism.

THANK YOU!

If this book has resonated with your heart, help other people discover it by writing a review or just leaving a rating wherever you bought it. Your voice is extremely important and powerful! This might take only a few minutes, yet it will make a huge difference in bringing this work to the attention of other readers.

Any effort to spread the word about this book would be greatly appreciated. Thank you!

If you would like to be kept up to date with our latest releases, please sign up for our newsletter at:

radiantbooks.co/bonus

ABOUT THE AUTHOR

MOTHER OF AGNI YOGA, **Helena Roerich** (1879–1955), proclaimed the dawn of the New Era and the future Resurrection of Spirit and Love in the world. From 1920 to 1947, she recorded another cycle of Divine Wisdom from the Great Teachers — *Agni Yoga*, also known as the *Teaching of Living Ethics*. It was written for the most part in countries of the East, in collaboration with the Lord of Shambhala. Aimed initially at the mind, this Fiery Teaching paves the way to the heart and points to Infinity in the Cosmos and in Life. Moreover, the Heroic Deed of Helena Roerich consisted not only in delivering the Teaching to humanity but also in the fact that she offered herself up for the Fiery Experiment — the influence of cosmic energies upon an individual incarnated in physical form. This Experiment has helped the Teachers of Humanity find ways to minimize the sufferings of the world in the present day, as these cosmic energies began to affect all humanity and planet Earth from 1999 onwards. By strictly following the canons and principles of the secret science, *Gupta-Vidya*, Roerich succeeded in mastering the cosmic Fire, and reached the highest condition of spirituality possible on Earth.

WORKS:
- **Agni Yoga Series**
- **Agni Yoga: The High Path**
- **On Eastern Crossroads**
- **Foundations of Buddhism**
- **Letters of Helena Roerich**
- **At the Threshold of the New World**

OTHER TITLES PUBLISHED BY RADIANT BOOKS

***The Land of the Gods* by H. P. Blavatsky.** Hidden in plain sight for 135 years, Blavatsky's story is a beautifully written account of an exceptional journey into Shambhala. Immersive and engaging, this profound book will provide you with a unique outlook on the deeper side of life, exposing our true nature, interior powers, and ultimate destiny. It explains grand, spiritual ideas more thoroughly and swiftly than any book you'll ever read.

***The Book of the Golden Precepts* by H. P. Blavatsky.** Full of incomparable beauty and inspirational power, this book reveals the Secret Path to Enlightenment followed by the greatest spiritual teachers of all time, such as Jesus Christ and Gautama Buddha. If you're seeking real spiritual growth, if you long to access divine wisdom that will explain everything that is happening in the world, if you want to live with deeper and majestic purpose, this book is your key.

***Revealing Cosmic Mysteries* by H. P. Blavatsky.** Lost for over a century, the full stenographic reports of meetings with Blavatsky in London have resurfaced recently. Immerse yourself in those very meetings at which Blavatsky revealed secret knowledge. The questions others posed may well have been your own, and her answers will unlock your deeper understanding of the Universe's profound secrets. You will be privy to Blavatsky's inspirational power, brilliant and penetrating mind, sharp wit and authentic wisdom.

***The Temple of Mysteries* by Francia La Due.** Bridging spirituality and science, this classic work is a true gem of the world's esoteric legacy. The Master Hilarion, the Protector of America and Europe, transmitted it through Francia La Due, intending to assist humanity in resolving the challenges of modern civilization and guide us toward unity with the cosmic forces that shape our existence. *The Temple of Mysteries* will illuminate your path to self-realization and help you find answers to the most pressing questions that trouble your soul.

***From the Mountaintop* by Francia La Due.** Uplifting and poetic, this book invites you to rediscover your true essence and forge a future illuminated by the light of resonant wisdom. It is a collection of high vibrational messages of truth and beauty that imbue the very aura of humanity. Transcending time and space, these messages radiate the healing energies of faith, hope, and love. For those who aspire to embark on the Path toward Mystery, *From the Mountaintop* will serve as a celestial beacon in troubled times.

***The Mystery of Christ* by Thales of Argos.** Eye-opening and heart-touching, *The Mystery of Christ* brings a fresh perspective, an uncommon insight, and spiritual depth to the dramatic events which occurred two thousand years ago. As you read the profoundly

OTHER TITLES PUBLISHED BY RADIANT BOOKS

stirring pages of this beautifully crafted narrative, you will comprehend the unequalled mission of Christ and the innermost secrets of Mary, culminating in an unexpected encounter with the new mystery of the Cosmos named Sophia.

The Living Waters of Joy by Grace Lucia Kimball. Through heartfelt revelations, this book will become your sanctuary — a spiritual oasis where your troubled soul can always find comfort, peace, and renewal, even in the most difficult of times. Like a healing balm, its eloquent prose flows as a gentle stream of living water, offering you a profound and uplifting experience of the Higher Presence.

The Song of Sano Tarot by Anna Fullwood. Unveiling the fundamentals of creation, this book relates the story of Seven Forces, or vibratory laws, that govern your life and the entire Universe. Each of us belongs to a particular vibration, and if you do not live in accordance with your natural force, you will reap negative consequences. From this viewpoint, the book offers insights and practical advice on how to determine your inherent force and transform your life, thereby guiding you toward inner balance and peace.

Becoming What You Are by Two Workers. Drawing on timeless spiritual wisdom, this book will take you on a journey toward self-realization and inner awakening. Its inspiring messages and practical advice will show you how to cultivate the qualities necessary for spiritual growth. It will help you align your actions with your highest potential and ultimately become what you are — a radiant and awakened being.

The Seven Laws of Spiritual Purity by Two Workers. Providing a profound and eye-opening perspective on achieving true spiritual purity, this thought-provoking and straightforward book draws practical advice from ancient wisdom to show you how to purify your mind, body, and soul. It is a passionate plea for a better world — a world in which humanity no longer has to accept and deal with the consequences of many sufferings but instead prevents their very causes.

The Kingdom of White Waters by V.G. For a thousand years, this secret story could be told only on the deathbed, for it revealed an inaccessible garden paradise hidden in the Himalayas — Shambhala, a place thousands of people searched for, but always failed to find. Each carrier of this secret story took a vow of silence that could be broken under only two conditions: when facing imminent death or in response to another's persistent requests for knowledge about the mythical Kingdom of White Waters.

∞

www.ingramcontent.com/pod-product-compliance
Lightning Source LLC
Chambersburg PA
CBHW060602080526
44585CB00013B/658